Saeed Sehizadeh was born in Iran and immigrated to the [...] high school. He earned a Masters Degree in Mechanical En[...] time, the defense industry went thru a shakedown and he worked as an engineer for two years. While he had enjoyed his Engineering education, he hated the work. By 1986, he had secured a job as a temporary employment counselor at a temp agency in Southern CA.

In 1988, George Herbert Bush became president. Bush immediately started to confront the problem of non-performing loans on the books of hundreds of Savings and Loans across the nation. The Federal agency tasked with dealing with the Savings and Loan problem was The Resolution Trust Corporation (RTC). The RTC was a US owned asset Management Company, charged with liquidating assets, primarily real estate related assets such as mortgage loans that had been assets of the savings and loan associations (S&Ls). Between 1989 and mid-1995, the Resolution Trust Corporation closed or otherwise resolved 747 thrifts with total assets of $394 billion.

The largest of those savings and loans was Gibraltar Savings in Simi Valley, CA, which would become the largest client of Mr. Sehizadeh's temp agency. He started the temp agency in 1989, shortly before the Federal Government took over the savings and loans industry. Because the Federal Government took over Gibraltar Savings, many of the existing employees left the company, necessitating the hiring of many temporary employees. Furthermore all of the loan portfolios in all savings and loans had to be evaluated to determine if they were performing or non-performing loans as a precondition for sale to investors.

Gibraltar Savings was not alone. Almost all savings and loans in Southern CA experienced the same problem: most of their loans were not performing. The problem was the result of these institutions' lending based on guidelines that didn't take into account the borrowers' capacity to pay back the loan. When the loans became non-performing, almost all savings and loans became insolvent, and the RTC took them over. Most of these institutions became Mr. Sehizadeh's clients and his temp agency provided the personnel to audit the loans as the RTC required.

By 1995, the savings and loan mess was coming to an end. The RTC was able to separate the performing and non-performing loans on the book of savings and loans. The Federal Government basically took over the non-performing loans and sold off the performing loans to banks.

This opened the door to the next chapter of Mr. Sehizadeh's temp agency where he filled temporary jobs at various banks across the nation. His main client was now Countrywide Financial, which would later become the largest subprime lender in the nation. It was during one of these jobs that he realized the looming unemployment disaster that was about to unfold.

By the year 2000, the Internet was starting to become visible and widely used. There were area of the country that still didn't have access, but it was now mainstream and quickly gaining ground.

Mr. Sehizadeh had placed a temporary employee at a bank in Southern CA. His job was to calculate the amortization data on various loans. Before he placed this employee on the job, about five or six employees were assigned the same task. To calculate the amortization of a loan, it took about half an hour to an hour to do the task, depending how mathematically inclined the worker was.

However, this enterprising employee had developed an algorithm on the web and was able to calculate the amortization data within minutes. The bank immediately fired all their other employees because this one employee was doing the job of six employees. When Mr. Sehizadeh discussed the matter with this employee, the employee explained how he'd been able to write a simple program at home, host it on his servers and use the program at work to expedite the calculation.

Mr. Sehizadeh realized this trend would continue and create unemployment in certain industries. It would be another 10 years before his fears manifested and many workers across the globe began losing their jobs. Fearing unemployment himself, Mr. Sehizadeh attended law school and went on to become an admitted member of the CA Bar in 2001.

By 2002, the banking industry was already shedding jobs and like many whose businesses had fed off of the subprime loan market, Mr. Sehizadeh was forced to shut down his temp agency. Subprime loans had become exceedingly common as the subprime lending criteria was non-existent. Regardless of the borrowers' ability to pay or his credit worthiness, they were given loans. These loans were then packaged and sold to Wall Street, to be sold to investors later.

By 2002, Mr. Sehizadeh realized he must own something on the web. After several failures, he started an Internet company that primarily served lawyers that is still active today.

In Oct of 2007, the stock market had once again made headlines as it was trading at record levels. The S & P was trading at about 1575. By then, the job market was showing signs of slowing down, though the government was denying any problem.

By March 2009, the market would tumble to half its value from its height. While the financial crisis and the faltering of the subprime loans have been offered as the culprit, the rationale remains faulty. While the financial crisis may have contributed to the decline in the market, it can't be the only reason. The Wall Street executives are not aware of this fact either. In the ensuing subpoenas and testimonies before the senate, not one of them offered the Internet as the reason for the demise.

It was in 2009 that Mr. Sehizadeh started this book: The Curse of the Internet, to shed some light on the real cause of unemployment. The politicians all agree that creating jobs is the main task at hand. Many propose cutting taxes to create jobs, while others suggest more absurd solutions. The reason such faulty logic is at play is because none of them understand that it is the Internet causing unemployment. Mr. Sehizadeh's book aims to provide that missing link.

The Curse
of the Internet

by

Saeed Sehizadeh

Copyright

© 2011 Saeed Sehizadeh

ISBN: 978-1467944564

For my daughter Sophia
who taught me how to love and how to forgive...

And let us remember that the Internet revolution will also pass and in the scheme of things this is just another blip in the evolution of our planet

End of all of time

Leaving me behind

Leading a moving line

Million Miles long

Acknowledgment

Special Thanks to Rob Schneider (www.writing-resources.org). He did much of the research for many of the articles and the final editing of the book. Most Chapter titles were suggested by him.

Contents

Introduction

In the early 19th century, a group of laborers, fearing the emerging industrial age was going to destroy their livelihoods and lead to misery for the masses, took it upon themselves to protest against mechanization by destroying machinery. One of these protesters, Ned Ludd, destroyed a knitting frame. Ludd is the man responsible for the name given to these "paranoid" workers: Luddites.

Since the industrial revolution seems to have led to the wealthiest era in human history, the Luddites have become something of a joke. Today, a Luddite is defined as a person who dislikes or is afraid or technology or is incompetent when using new technologies. The theory put forward by the Luddites, that technology would replace jobs, is derisively referred to as the "Luddite Fallacy". The Luddites got it wrong, according to the pundits, by not seeing the upside of mechanization. Yes, jobs were initially lost, but the prices of goods dropped dramatically. This in turn led to greater consumption. Greater consumption led to greater production in existing and new industries. This in turn led to more jobs, greater prosperity and increased living standards for everyone.

There are some holes in this argument, though. Industrialization drastically reduced the need for agricultural laborers. This hit blacks in the American south hard. They migrated north to find jobs. For many, there were no jobs to be found and that was the beginning of the urban ghettoes. Similarly, since mechanization and automation, the so-called "Rust Belt", the industrial Northeast, Mid-Atlantic and eastern parts of the Midwest, have some of the highest levels of unemployment in the United States. Mechanization and automation did not create lasting job opportunities for those millions of workers.

Still, until the economic crisis that began in 2007 arrived, America and the rest of the world was on a roll and gave the new technologies much credit for that roll. As it turns out, the "credit" for all the seeming prosperity had to go to easy credit and other unsound economic factors. Regardless of the wisdom of the bailouts and other financial strategies that have been taken to improve the economy, jobs remain scarce. While the stock market revived in 2009-2010, employment continued to stagnate: as an article on CNN's Money site put it in 2010; *Poof: Another 800,000 jobs disappear.* The article points out while approximately 7 million jobs were lost in 2007-2008, the figure edged up to close to eight million in 2009, with no signs of improvement in sight. What happened to the "recovery"?

One person who is in a position to know is Martin Ford. With over a quarter of a century in the computer design and software development fields and as a successful Silicon Valley entrepreneur, Ford is a technology insider. Unlike many of his peers, Martin Ford believes that the technological revolution will displace even more jobs than the industrial revolution did and that it will hit all employment sectors.

While Martin Ford and others are looking into the future, the current employment crisis strongly suggests that this "Neo-Luddite" future is already upon us and that those who sagely cite the "Luddite Fallacy" are living in the past: their arguments don't hold up in a post-industrial society. While mechanization and industrialization created enough new jobs to employ millions of blue collar workers and a whole new class of white collar workers; the internet, digital or technological revolution (call it what you like), is not only destroying jobs in traditional sectors of the economy, it is destroying tech jobs as well.

In 2003, CIO, an online financial magazine, published *Robert Reich on Technology's Impact on Job Loss in America.* In this article, Reich, the Secretary of Labor during the Clinton administration, was concerned because IT employment in the U.S. had shrunk by 20% in the two years since 2001. Reich cited three reasons for this. One of these was obvious: the bursting of the dotcom bubble. The others were not so obvious at the time. As Reich said: "enormous productivity gains brought on by IT itself has, ironically, reduced the need for many midlevel project managers." He then went on to say that while outsourcing was a factor, it was "a small factor relative to the bad economy and the productivity gains wrought by automation."

In 2009, Reich was still concerned about technology's effect on the job market. In his blog, he commented on *The Great Disconnect*

Between Stocks and Jobs with these words: "How can the stock market hit new highs at the same time unemployment is hitting new highs? Simple. The market is up because corporate earnings are up. Corporate earnings are up because companies are cutting costs. And the biggest single cost they're cutting is their payrolls." He backed up his claim by citing the surprising profits shown by Caterpillar Corporation. In the 3rd quarter of 2009, the company earned $404 million. This amounted to 64 cents per share, as opposed to analysts' predictions of just 5 cents. "How did Caterpillar do it?" he asked and then answered his own question: "It did it by cutting over 37,000 jobs."

How many of those jobs are going to be absorbed by the giants of the internet?

Google: In late January, 2011, Google announced it was going to hire another 6,200 employees over the course of the year. That's good news until you look a little closer at the statistics. With a total of around 40,000 employees scattered throughout 60 offices in 30 different countries, Google's revenues in 2010 were over $29 billion. This was up $7 billion from the previous year, yet the company needed only six thousand additional employees worldwide. The company declined to comment on how the new jobs were going to be distributed, but did mention that it expected around 1000 of them to go to Europe. When you consider the probable spread of the other 5000 throughout roughly two dozen other countries, Google's "hiring frenzy" was not that impressive. Google investors, however, grumbled about the negative effect it would have on company profits.that the company was adding too much staff and that they would eat into company profits. As Tommy Stevenson of the Tuscaloola News put it: "Now this is just insane (and un-American)". One thing is for sure: Google is not going to put much of a dent in the jobs lost at Caterpillar.

EBay: EBay is another internet success story. Between this online auction house and its PayPal subsidiary, the company made over $9 billion in revenue in 2008. This was an increase of 11% over the previous year, in spite of the recession. 2009 saw EBay's profits jump a further 19%. In March of 2008, EBay employed 15,500 workers. At the end of December, 2009, the company employed 16,400 and this included temps. This "growth" of 900 employees after achieving such massive growth in revenues is hardly anything to get excited about.

Oracle: Oracle is a computer technology company, headquartered in California with offices around the world. The company specializes in creating and marketing enterprise software products and hardware systems. Some of Oracle's products include the Oracle database, Open Office, PeopleSoft, and Sun Microsystems.

In 2008, Oracle earned $5.3 billion in revenue and had 84,233 employees. By December 31, 2010, the company had 105,000 full time employees and made $31.99 billion in revenue. In other words, while the company's profits soared nearly six-fold, its number of employees grew by less than 20%.

Amazon: The Amazon phenomenon puts to rest any speculation that jobs lost in the retail sector due to internet competition will be made up for in internet and high tech jobs. In December, 2009, Amazon had 24,300 full time and part time employees. These employees are spread out over 25 "fulfillment centers" around the world. By the end of 2010, this number increased by 6,900 to 31,200. In the same period of time, Amazon's net sales were up by 46.1%. Any pre-digital age company with growth like that would require an enormous increase in staff, yet a quick look at its Career Opportunities page on May 02, 2011 showed that Amazon needed only 696 new employees throughout the United States. 549 of these were at the company's Seattle headquarters.

Amazon's growth came at a price to its competitors. When Borders Books declared bankruptcy in 2011, after massive job cuts and structural changes failed to reverse the downward spiral in company revenues that began in 2006, it announced the closure of up to 275 retail outlets. Borders was hesitant to say how many jobs were going, but it's a safe bet that Amazon, the company that is generally held responsible for Borders' bankruptcy, didn't have enough positions open to take up the slack.

Google, EBay, Oracle and Amazon are just three examples of why the Luddites may have just been ahead of their time. As subsequent chapters of this book reveal, the technological advances of the late 20th century and 21st century offer businesses in all sectors of the economy the opportunity to increase profits by cutting back on their workforce. Where new employees are needed, they are found wherever they can be bought for the cheapest price. In the United States and other developed countries, this has already led to drastic salary and benefits cuts. In the year 2000, for example, a senior software engineer could expect to earn up to $130,000 per year. By 2003, the salary was already down to less than $100,000. It was worse for entry level help desk employees, whose salaries dropped from $55,000 to $35,000 in the same time period. While these salary levels have remained stable since then, the cost of living has not, so in real dollar terms, they have fallen even further.

While the displaced workers in the 19th century Industrial Revolution eventually found employment in industry and as education became widespread, new opportunities arose for workers in white collar jobs, the situation is not quite the same in the brave new world of the internet. In the Industrial Revolution, jobs involving manual labor increased along with productivity. At the same time, jobs requiring mental skills increased because there was no alternative to the human brain. Computer technology has already advanced to the point where millions of white collar jobs have become unnecessary and software engineers are making computers and the internet smart enough to replace many of their own jobs. Where they are not replaced, they are not creating jobs as rapidly as the internet destroys them. Martin Ford and others believe that thanks to technological advancements, machines are rapidly outpacing humans in their ability to perform both manual and mental tasks. In his view and that of others, the inevitable consequence of this will be massive unemployment. These are just a few examples of why Ford's prediction is already coming to pass:

Retail

Shopping malls are going bankrupt and as the recession eases (whether temporarily or not), they are not being snapped up by speculators looking for bargains because shopping centers are no longer being considered viable investments. Virtually all of the large department chains are investing in their online presence and reducing or eliminating altogether their investments in new brick and mortar stores. Many are even closing non-performing outlets and writing off their losses.

How many once thriving retail businesses are closing their doors and going online? Wallet Pop is a consumer finance site that ran a special report on retail closures throughout America in 2009. Their list of closures was a long one. Just a few of them included household names like these:

* Payless Shoes planned on closing 67 outlets in 2009
* Zales Jewelry shut down 191 stores in the first half of 2009
* Blockbuster Video planned on shedding up to 960 outlets by the end of 2011, citing pressure from online services like Netflix
* Bath and Body chain Crabtree & Evelyn filed for bankruptcy in 2009. This company, founded in 1973, now has less stores and a stronger online presence
* Sears Holdings announced the closer of a further 22 Kmart and 6 Sears stores in 2009
* Jones Apparel planned on closing 225 stores between 2009-2011

These few examples illustrate that the closing of retail stores is not limited to just one or two business niches. The closures continue and the internet is the main culprit. On February 16, 2011, for example, Borders Books filed for Chapter 11 bankruptcy. In her coverage of the story, *Wallet Pop* reporter Laura Heller remarked that, "simply put, Borders failed to get in front of the shift to digital content."

Manufacturing

In 2008, the robotics industry was hit as hard by the recession as other industries were. Interestingly, though, this industry recovered more quickly than others. An upturn was noticed as early as 2009 and 2010 turned out to be a very good year for robotics. Why was this so? It was because recovering warehouses and factories, after laying off tens of thousands of workers in the early stages of the recession, determined that increasing their investment in robotics was more cost effective and efficient than rehiring workers. If a manufacturing plant or warehouse lays off 100 workers during a recession and only hires back 25 of them after the recession because they "hired" robots instead, where are the other 75 workers going to find jobs? It's not going to be at the bailed out auto manufacturers: they have been the heaviest investors in robotics.

Financial Services

Over 80,000 stockbrokers lost their jobs on Wall Street alone during the recession and they are not getting them back. Why? Because investors found better service and cheaper prices online and financial service companies are replacing stockbrokers with online brokerless trading services. In the banking sector, banks have been actively reducing staff levels since before internet banking became available. Ever since the introduction of ATMs (Automated Teller Machines), banks have been cutting back on opening new branches. Why open a new branch and employ human tellers when *Automated* Tellers can do the job quicker, more efficiently and at a far cheaper cost? As online banking services improve and consumers grow accustomed to them, the need for brick and mortar banks and human staff members continues to shrink.

Bank of America, one of America's oldest and most respected banks still had 5856 branches at the close of 2010, but that was down 2.6% from the previous year. The bank has plans in place to shed another 10% of its branches and are planning on transforming another 10% into "Merrill Lynch Specialty Stores" that will be manned by "a small-business adviser or mortgage expert, or video links to those representatives." Note the use of the singular: one person will replace the dozens who were formerly employed by the bank or perhaps customers will just sit down and talk to a video display.

Printing and Publishing

It seems like every day you read about another venerable newspaper closing its doors forever after having been printing newspapers for over a hundred years. The big publishing houses are now in the position of having to negotiate with Amazon over the price they can charge for digital versions of their books. They can't refuse to negotiate because digital devices like the Amazon Kindle have caught on with the buying public, while printed book sales are in decline. Those people who still buy printed books are buying them online from Amazon instead of in book stores. The big booksellers like Barnes and Noble are fighting back in the only way they can - online. They are closing the doors of their retail outlets and investing in their online stores and, in the case of Barnes and Noble, releasing its own digital reading device.

When a publishing house or newspaper goes broke or goes online, it sheds jobs, but that's only the beginning of the story. Those who are employed by the printing companies lose their jobs as well and in fact have been doing so for years, ever since the advent of digital printing made it possible to cut staff in printing houses to virtually nothing. Further down the supply line, fewer pulp mills are needed, so many thousands more jobs in rural areas are lost. Once a pulp mill is closed, the workers move on and an entire town that once thrived on the business provided by the workers in the mill faces unemployment.

The Curse of the Internet

"May you live in interesting times" is said to be an ancient Chinese curse. Times of upheaval and change are "interesting times" that take an enormous toll on human welfare and stability. The internet age is definitely an interesting time to be alive. The purpose of this book is to awaken us to the current affects of the internet and our prospects for the future. Together, maybe we can find some solutions to the problems that face us.

1
Robots Creating a Meltdown of Manufacturing Jobs

The manufacturing sector is one of the key fields where robots are fast replacing human labor. The US Department classifies the manufacturing sector into 10 categories. All these various categories have been the traditional employers of a considerable proportion of the labor force. The US manufacturing sector as a whole is comprised of about 290,000 establishments, including both small, single location companies and large multi location companies, with total combined annual sales of $5 trillion. In 2000, manufacturing industries accounted for 17% of the US GDP. In 2005, before the recession, it was down to 14.4%. This reduction of manufacturing has been a consistent trend in the US manufacturing industries, especially in this decade. This reduction in production, combined with increased automation, resulted in an annual job loss figure in the manufacturing sector of approximately 3% between the years 2000 and 2007, the latest year data is available.

The futuristic vision of a world where robots perform tasks formerly undertaken only by humans as depicted in science fiction and film is fast becoming a reality in the manufacturing sector. The automobile industry, for instance, depends largely on highly precise and efficient robotic manufacturing units that have replaced their less capable human counterparts. The result for the human work force, of course, has been increasing unemployment. While this is devastating for workers, it is ideal for manufacturers, who no longer need to worry about minimum wages, health insurance or any of the other inconveniences posed by a human workforce. When a robot is also able to outperform its human counterpart, there is little incentive for manufacturers not to turn to robotic applications.

The correlation between unemployment and robotics became strikingly evident in 2010 when, after the drastic labor cuts that followed the recession in 2008-2009, there was a disproportionate increase in sales of robots versus increased job opportunities. In response to the increased demand, industrial robots are evolving fast to incorporate advanced robotics features like machine vision and finger sensitivity, thus offering even smarter options to manufacturers. For instance, there is the pi4 Workerbot, introduced at the Vision 2010 meet in Stuttgart. This stand alone lightweight industrial robot (only 500kg) is placed on a rolling platform for flexible implementation. The robot is equipped with two state of the art inspection cameras on either side of its head, and a third optional time-of-flight camera to gather a 3D image of the work piece on which its working and make intelligent inferences about it. The robot is capable of precision handling of fragile materials and can transfer of the work piece from one robotic hand to another. The Workerbot is even capable of making facial expressions, to make it more engaging to human workers. It can engage in a variety of tasks, including assembly, sorting, quality control and hazardous tasks.

While robots are not likely to entirely supplant human workers, manufacturers are increasingly using them, both for practical reasons and to enhance their corporate identity. A company that uses advanced robotics is considered to be an advanced, forward thinking company. This has been evident throughout the forty years since industry began using the first robots, but in the United States, their implementation has been hampered somewhat due to pressure from trade unions and other public employment advocates. For this reason, Japan, Germany and other European countries already have surpassed the US in the use of robotics technology, especially in the automobile industry. The recession and the bankruptcy of US automobile manufacturers led to a relaxation of many of the regulations that protected workers' rights in the past, so it is likely that US auto makers are going to increasingly use robots instead of human labor.

The importance of robots is not limited to the automobile industry. Other large manufacturing industries such as the electronics industry, the food and beverage manufacturing industry and the plastic industry are also developing an increasing reliance on robots to perform the tasks that were until now performed by human hands.

Indeed, robots are even being used in hundreds of industries outside the manufacturing industry. For example, robots are being used in the field of medicine to perform critical surgical operations or to work as the surgeon's assistant in the operations. Another field of conspicuous application of robotics is being found in the military, where the robots are replacing human soldiers in lethal situations, such as bomb defusion. Unmanned aerial aircrafts and ground vehicles are increasingly being used by the military for surveillance of enemy areas. The SpeciMinder, a robot developed by Swisslog Healthcare Solutions and CCS robotics, cleans hallways and doors without walking by pre-specified guides embedded in the floor. The SpeciMinder will even ask for help using a voice signal if it finds someone blocking its path! A similar robot developed by researchers at UC Berkeley has been taught how to fold towels and other non-rigid items. Then there is EMILY, the robotic lifeguard designed to rescue drowning people, patrolling beaches and remote-operated by a human lifeguard from the shore. While these applications outside of the manufacturing industries may not directly affect jobs in the manufacturing sector, the technologies developed for these applications are being adapted to manufacturing and are just one more sign of things to come.

The demand for robots is a global phenomenon. Asian countries like China and South Korea are rapidly turning to robotic technology for manufacturing applications. In fact, the demand from Asian economies has been one of the main reasons for the unprecedented hike in robot units sold in 2010. The continuously rising use of robots in different industries is another indicator that robots are destined to replace humans in the manufacture of goods. Increasingly, a company that does not employ robotics is a company that cannot compete in the global marketplace.

Robots in the Manufacturing Sector

In the beginning, robots were incorporated into the manufacturing sector to perform tasks that were too dangerous, difficult or tediously repetitious for humans to perform efficiently and safely. However, this has changed and robots are replacing human labor in almost all areas of manufacturing. Though some aspects of manufacturing still require the dexterity of human hands and the intelligence of a human mind, as robotics research progresses, there are fewer and fewer tasks robots cannot perform as well as or better than humans.

The programmability of industrial robots and their ability to perform complex manufacturing tasks with speed and precision are making them the preferred replacement for human labor. The fact that employing the robots does not include traditional employment responsibilities like social security and retirement plans is also a major reason why industry leaders prefer them to human labor. As more companies are adapting to automation, the competition is compelling other companies to tread the same path. Robots are now "employed" in various stages of production, from assembly to palletizing and spray painting. This is why, following the job cuts of the recession, many manufacturing companies decided to invest in new robotic systems rather than hiring people. The robots easily accomplish manufacturing tasks like welding, assembling, cutting and polishing with minimal error. The only human participation in these robotic units is limited to supervision and maintenance of the robotic units, since robots are yet to be able to perform these tasks on their own.

Apart from possible operational problems, working with robots still has certain limitations. For instance, robots can be programmed to perform a particular task under specified conditions. However, if there is any change in these specified conditions, the robot finds itself at loss to adapt to the changed circumstances. The robot has to be then reprogrammed to perform under the changed work conditions. This requires certain advanced features in the robots and all robots cannot be as easily reprogrammed as human workers can be retrained. Reprogramming is an expensive process and not a cost-effective one. In addition, since robots lack native intelligence, actions that are easy for human workers are extremely complex for a robot. Artificial intelligence is yet to replace human intelligence. Take for instance, the pi4 Workerbot. This is one of the most advanced robots available right now and an action as simple as transferring an object from one hand to another is actually a breakthrough accomplishment for the robot.

While the fact that robots cannot yet perform all the highly complex tasks that humans can may seem to bode well for workers in the manufacturing sector, major US manufacturers continue to train and use cheaper offshore labor, thus eroding the labor market in the United States even more.

History of Industrial Robots

The term 'robot' can be traced back to Czech word 'robota' that translates as compulsory labor or serfdom. This term is said to have been first used in 1921 in a Czech play 'R.U.R' (Rossum's Universal Robots), by Karel Capek. The play was about humanoid robots that eventually destroyed their human makers; a theme still explored in recent science fiction movies like I, Robot in 2004. The idea of programmable machinery, however, stretches back much earlier, to the 18th century. In the 1720s, Frenchmen Bouchon, Basile, Vacaunson, Falcon and Jacquard were able to develop mechanical looms that were controlled by punch cards. Another one of these earliest developments was in 1892, when Seward Babbitt of Pittsburgh was able to obtain a patent for a rotary crane with motorized gripper, designed for removing ingots out of furnaces. In 1933, Pollard developed a jointed mechanical arm that could repeat a series of movements. This machine was designed for spray painting, a function for which industrial robots are extensively used today. These machines were developed to assist humans with their work and not replace them. This largely remained the trend throughout much of the 20th century, but with new developments in the field of robotics, robots are increasing replacing rather than assisting human workers.

An important milestone in the history of robotics was in 1954, when George Devol developed the first general purpose manipulator with point-to-point control and playback memory. Devol received a patent for his Programmed Article Transfer in 1961. The patent states, "Universal Automation, or "Unimation", is a term that may well characterize the general object of this invention". Devol sold his patent to Condec and it formed the base of Condec's robot division, Unimation, Inc. Between 1954 and 1963, Devol and several others proceeded to make patents for their first generation of robots. Unimation, Inc. was founded by Devol and Joseph. F. Engelberger in 1956.

The first generation of Programmable Transfer Machines was able to transfer objects from one place to another. They used hydraulic actuators and were "joint coordinates programmed": their joints were specified coordinates during the training phase, which was repeated by these machines with extreme accuracy. The accuracy of these machines was in the range of 1/10,000 of an inch. Unimation later entered into a manufacturing deal with two companies, Kawasaki Heavy Industries in Japan and Guest-Nettlefolds in England, who started manufacturing the Unimates.

In the beginning, Unimation's only competitor was Ohio based firm Cincinnati Milacron Inc. However, this changed radically later in the late 1970s when several big Japanese conglomerates began producing industrial robots. This increase in competition fueled the development of industrial robots which further aided in the replacement of human labor in factories.

The next phase of robotics research marked the transition from "hard wired" robots to computer controlled "soft wired" robots. The early robots had electronic logic components that were 'hard wired' to perform a specific task. Researchers at the Stanford Research Institute developed an experimental robot called SHAKEY in 1968. SHAKEY was able to move and arrange blocks into stacks, assisted by a television camera and a computer.

The next milestone in robotics was in 1969, when Victor Scheinman of Stanford University developed the Robotic arm called the Stanford Arm, which was a 6 axis, electrical robot designed to provide an arm solution. This was a significant milestone in the development of robots as the arm was able to follow arbitrary paths in space. Scheinman designed a second arm for the MIT AI lab, and called it the "MIT Arm". Consequently, Scheinman received a fellowship from Unimation to further develop his designs and sold the designs to Unimation. Unimation further worked on these designs with assistance from General Motors and later marketed it as the PUMA or the Programmable Universal Machine for Assembly.

Robots controlled by general purpose computers were developed in the early 1970s. Cincinnati Milacron was the first company to commercialize the first mini computer controlled robot in 1974. In 1973, the first computer integrated robot assembly station was developed at Stanford. A three-legged walking machine was developed at the University of Wisconsin in 1974. The participation of General Motors in the robotics research showed clearly how the automobile industry was aware of the industrial potential of robotic production.

Types of Industrial Robots

Five main categories of robots are being employed by the industrial sector. These include:

1) Cartesian or Gantry Robots
2) Selective Compliant Articulated Robot Arm (SCARA) Robots
3) Cylindrical Robots
4) Polar Robots
5) Delta or Parallel Kinematic Robots

A Cartesian robot configuration, also known as a rectilinear configuration, can move along three Cartesian coordinates x, y and z. The gantry robot may also be equipped with an attached wrist to allow for rotational movement. The three prismatic joints of the robotic arm are capable of delivering a linear motion along the axis.

A SCARA robot configuration includes two horizontal joints and a cylindrical work area. A SCARA robot is designed to provide precision in a single plane rather than working in multiple planes. The SCARA robots are generally used in assembly applications.

A cylindrical robot configuration is similar to a SCARA robot as it also features a cylindrical work area. However, unlike a SCARA robot, the robotic arm is connected with one rotary joint at the base, with the arm's links connected by linear joints. The rotary joint moves in a rotational axis while the prismatic joints move in a linear fashion.

In a polar robotic configuration, the robotic arm is connected to the robotic base by a twisted joint and to a combination of two rotary joints and a linear joint. The work area of a polar robot is spherical.

The spider like delta robots are comprised of jointed parallelograms connected to a common base. The parallelograms together create a dome shaped working area. The delta robots are capable to be used in the food, pharmaceutical and the electronic industry as it can be programmed to perform delicate and precise movements.

Of these, the SCARA robots and the Cartesian robots are those that are most in demand. The SCARA robots still are mostly used in the electronics sector, although the Cartesian robots are fast catching up too. The Cartesian robots possess a definite advantage of more closely imitating a human arm where automation from manual labor is an important prerequisite for robotic participation. The common factor connecting each type of robot is that they are all responsible for replacing human labor in the factories and are doing so increasingly.

Industrial robots are also classified according to the type of path they generate. The robots are programmed from the control panel to generate one of the following three paths.

Point to Point Path: Such robots are programmed to move from one discrete point to another within the robot's working envelope. However, in the automatic mode of operation, the exact path followed by the robot can vary due to mechanical errors, variation in velocity among different components of the robot, joint geometries and point spatial locations. This difference in path can pose potential safety hazards to workers within the robotic work envelope.

Controlled Path: This ensures that the end of the robotic arm will follow a controlled path in a point-to-point movement. The risk of safety hazards is significantly less in controlled path programming.

Continuous Path: The path of the robot in this case is controlled by a large number of spatial points in close succession that is stored in the memory of the robot during a teaching sequence. When the robot is placed in the automatic mode of operation from the teach mode, the program is replayed from memory to generate a duplicate path.

Parts of an Industrial Robot

In order to get a complete understanding of how robots can be helpful in the industry, it is necessary to know exactly how a robot does the operations that they are programmed to do. The parts of an industrial robot include the controller, the end effector, the drive and the sensor, apart from the obvious and functional robotic arm.

The Controller: The controller is the computer "brain" of the robot and controls the actions of the different parts of the robot and is also programmed to connect the robot to other computerized systems. A teach pendant installs the program in the controller. A *teach pendant* is a handheld application that is used with a robotic controller to program and operate an industrial robot. The teach pendant normally possesses a keypad, a display and an emergency stop switch. The programming language of the teach pendant varies with the controller and the manufacturer, although most teach pendants run on operating systems similar to Windows operating system.

The Robotic Arm: Like the human arm, the robotic arm is also made up of a series of joints. The joints connect different metallic segments called the shoulder, the elbow and the wrist. The controller initiates the movement of the robotic arm by rotating the individual step motors connected to each arm joint. In large robots, sometimes hydraulics or pneumatics are also used for joint control. Generally, robotic arms have three degrees of freedom that allow six different movement planes for the robot. The majority of industrial robots used in manufacturing units today are six axis robots, capable of moving up and down; forward and backward; and left and right.

The End Effector: The end effector is the robotic 'hand' that is connected to the robotic arm and is designed for multiple purposes.

An end effector can be a gripper, a vacuum pump, a welding torch and other similar parts connected to a robot to do its job. The end effector is also provided with a sense of touch by the inbuilt load-cells in it. These load cells can judge the force applied by the industrial robot to grip a particular object. The robot operator can thereby set the force to prevent it from either breaking or dropping the object it is handling.

The Drive: The drive refers to the *step motor* that is connected to the joints of the robotic arm. Step motors are different from ordinary motors in that that they are capable of moving in exact increments, thus making precise movements possible in repeated cycles. Hydraulic drives are used when the robot is designed to lift heavy loads and perform at high speeds. Hydraulic drives can easily enable the robot to lift loads in excess of 500 pounds. Moreover, the hydraulic drives are preferred in volatile gas environments, where an electric motor poses a risk of explosions. However, hydraulic drives are prone to oil leakage that can be a potential fire hazard. The hydraulic drives are less suited for indoor application where the robots are in close proximity to the operating personnel. An electric drive system provides less speed and strength, but increased precision. The pneumatic drive systems are used for smaller robots that have fewer movement axes.

Sensors: Robotic sensors allow the robot to receive feedback from its working environment. The sensors allow limited senses of sound and sight to the robots. The sensor sends the feedback to the controller by electronic impulses after collecting it from the environment. Robotic sensors are also used to prevent two robots working adjacent to each other from bumping into each other. Sensors also help the robot to decide which items to pick up and which to ignore.

The physical sensors of an industrial robot can be classified into two categories, *active sensors* and *passive sensors*. The active sensors are those that emit physical energy and receive feedback by judging the interaction of the signals with the environment. Ultrasonic, laser and IR sensors are examples of active sensors. The passive sensors are those that receive energy already in the environment. Passive sensors consume less energy than active sensors, but they often have noise and signal problems. A robotic camera is an example of a passive sensor that works as the "eyes" of the robot.

Robots also need a power source. The energy is provided to robot actuators and the controllers as pneumatic, hydraulic and electrical. The selection of the power source is generally based on the application of the robot. Pneumatic power (low-pressure air) is generally used for low weight carrying robots, while hydraulic power (high-pressure oil) is preferred for medium to high force or weight applications. Electrically powered robots, both AC and DC, are most common in the industry.

Programming an Industrial Robot

The programming of an industrial robot is essential for the robot to perform the tasks specified to it. The setup or programming of an industrial robot is typically done by linking the robot controller to a laptop or desktop computer. An action as simple as putting the nut on the screw will require instructions for every single step of the action. The robot must be guided to how to hold the nut, how to find a collision free path to the screw and how to put the nut on the screw. In fact, this is an aspect of robotics where human effort is still unmatched by a robot. Nevertheless, in hazardous work environments where human employees may find it dangerous to work, industrial robots can be employed effectively to perform the action. In addition, the robot is also employed in production areas where a high speed is required to perform repeated work cycles.

The robot and the collection of machines in the work area of the robot is referred to as the cell or the work cell. For instance, a typical work cell might consist of a parts feeder, a molding machine and the robot. The various machines and the robot are integrated and controlled by a single computer or the PLC (Programmable Logic Controller). The corresponding interface software is installed in the computer. The robot software is run either in the robot controller, or in the computer or in both depending upon the system design.

There are two basic aspects of robot programming, positional data and the procedure. The robot software controls both these programming tasks. The robot can be programmed by one of the following methods depending on the design of the robot.

Teach Method: 90% of the industrial robots are programmed by the teach method. A handheld controlled programming unit or a teach pendant is used in this method. A teach pendant can be used to manually place the robot in different positions or adjust itself in a desired position. The teach pendant also consists of means to change the speed as low speed is required for careful positioning of the robot. A large emergency stop button or the dead man's handle is always included in the teach pendant. The teach pendant is used to manually drive the robot in a number of different coordinate systems locations. These coordinate locations are then stored with programming names so that the robot can follow the same path in repeated actions. The different coordinate systems available in a standard robotic arm are as follows:

Joint coordinates: The robotic joints are independently driven in either direction.

Global coordinates: The tool center point of the robot can be driven along the X, Y or Z axes of the global axis of the robot. Rotations of the tool around these axes can also be performed.

Tool coordinates: the axis of movement is placed at the tool center point of the robot and therefore move with it. This is the preferred coordinate system in robots where the tool centre point of the robot is near the work piece.

Work piece coordinates: some robot designs enable the robots to set up a coordinate system in any point within its workspace. In effect, this is similar to moving and positioning the global coordinate system of the robot.

Lead Through the Nose Method: This method was initially very popular among robot designers, but now it is less commonly used. In this method, one operator physically holds the robot's manipulator, while another operator enters a command to de-energize the robot, causing it to go limp. The first operator then moves the robot to the desired positions by hand along the required path and the software logs these positions into the robotic memory. The program can later run the robot to the desired path automatically. This method is popular in programming paint spraying robots. However, any hesitations or inaccuracies in the program cannot be reprogrammed easily, so this method requires at least two experienced robotic operators. Also, while carrying out this process, precautions should be taken to ensure the safety of the first operator from any erratic behavior of the robot.

Off line Programming: In this method, the entire cell in the workspace is mapped graphically in the robotic software interface. The robot can then be moved on screen and the process will be simulated. However, this method has limited value because it depends on the positional accuracy of the robot, which may not conform to what is programmed.

The Demand for Robotics in 2010

According to a November 2010 statistical report from the International Federation of Robotics (IFR), more than 100,000 industrial robots were sold worldwide in 2010. Such unprecedented sales surprised even the IFR, which had earlier set an expected timeline up to 2013 to achieve such numbers. In fact, the first nine months of 2010 witnessed a twofold sale of robotic units compared to 2009. The IFR attributes increasing demand from consumer markets and the sharp competition to meet this demand as the reasons behind this extraordinary increase in sales. The stress on eco-friendly production units also fuelled the sale of robots, according to IFR. IFR president Ake Lindqvist additionally referred to an accumulated demand for robotics during the financial recession of 2009 as a key reason of increasing sale of robot units in 2010. Although Mr. Lindqvist did not specify the exact nature of the accumulated demand, it can be assumed that he was referring to the labor reduction in various industries in 2009.

The car manufacturers and the electronics industry were the key drivers of the increased demand for robotics in 2010. The rising requirement of light weight manufacturing material, such as plastic, also fuelled the demand curve for industrial robots in 2010. As plastics are being used in building houses, cars and medical equipments, the robots are being engaged more than ever in different stages of production in the industry. Besides the automobile, the electronics, the plastics and the medical industries, industrial robots were also engaged more in the metal industry in 2010. It is noteworthy that these sales were not limited to the United States, but were a global phenomenon.

The IFR statement quoted Dr. Andreas Bauer, Chairman of the IFR Industrial Robots Suppliers Group, KUKA, Germany, as saying, "The dynamic development of robot sales intensified again in the third quarter in Europe. In the first half, particularly the car manufacturers bought high volumes of units, but in the third quarter also the demand from all other industries increased noticeably." The Executive director of Japan Robot Association (JARA) confirmed the accelerating demand from the Asian market of automobile and electronic industries, particularly from China.

This growth in the Asian markets, specifically China, is in fact a continuation of a trend that has been emerging for the last 4-5 years. According to another IFR survey report of 2007, the sale of robotic manufacturing units continued to rise in China, India, Malaysia and Taiwan in 2006 despite an overall fall in sales figures by 19% in 2006. The Chinese industries witnessed an increase by 29% in 2006, mainly in the automobile and the electronics industry, for both domestic and offshore investors in China. As of 2007, there were over 951,000 operational robots in various industries, with above 50 % of the total numbers in Asia, one third in Europe and 16% in North America.

The recession of 2009 caused a significant decrease in the number of robotic units sold worldwide. In fact, the number of robots sold fell by 47% (60,000 units) and reached an all time low since 1994, according to the statistics released by the IFR. However, 2010 saw an increased sale of robotic units and this trend is expected to continue between 2010 and 2013.

Functions and Advantages of Industrial Robots

The key factors contributing to the widespread use of robots in various fields include their abilities to perform repetitious tasks, operate in hazardous environments and their speed. Moreover, manufacturers find robots convenient to work with, because there is no need dispense a monthly wage or face any worker issues whatsoever. Robots do not get tired, sick, disgruntled or distracted. Sometimes they might temporarily stop working because of a mechanical malfunction, but this is infrequent and robot operators and technicians keep a close watch on them to prevent this from happening. Moreover, the quality of the parts produced by robotic technology is considered far superior to those produced by human labor.

Robotics in the Automobile Industry

The automobile industry is one of the largest employers of robots. Robots perform almost all the tasks in an automobile industry and human labor is often limited to robotic maintenance and supervision. Some of the processes they are used for include assembling the car parts, spot and arc welding, machine tending, laser processing, testing, crash testing, spray painting, sealing and dispensing.

An evaluation of the automobile industry is critical to an understanding of the extent of current and future robotic involvement in manufacturing as a whole. The inclusion of robots in the automobile industry began in the days of robotic boom in the 1980s and has continued at a steady rate. The shift towards robotics, in fact, was largely responsible for Japan's increasing dominance of the automotive industry in the 80s, when robot were more successfully integrated into the manufacturing process there. Robots provided Japanese carmakers with a solution to the problem of high labor costs, since Japanese workers could only be enticed to work in the automobile industry in exchange for prohibitively high wages. Moreover, Japan was able to accommodate the displaced workers from the automobile industry with other jobs, thus avoiding a decrease in consumer demand.

Although the US was the first country to manufacture robots, Japanese manufacturers more aggressively developed and marketed the technology, bringing the price of robotic applications down to a more affordable level in that country. The US on the other hand was forced to introduce robots gradually in their car production system, as unionized workers were vigorously opposed to them. The pressure to compete with Japan led the US administration to undertake policy changes that led to drastic unemployment in the automobile sector of the economy, but unlike Japan, was unable to accommodate the displaced workers. As a result, there was large-scale unemployment that consequently led to an economic crisis in the US. This in turn created a significant decrease in sales of US made vehicles and Japanese auto manufacturers moved in to fill in the vacuum. Since then, Japan and America have been highly competitive in the employment of industrial robots in the automotive industry.

Considerable research is being continuously directed towards more efficient application of robots in the automobile industry. One of the regions where robots are extensively used in the automobile industry is in the welding process on the assembly line. Thousands of spot welds are performed on a car body, as are a limited number of arc welds. A spot weld essentially involves running a very high electric current through overlapping metal pieces so that enough heat is created by the resistance to melt the metals and fuse them together. Spot welding is a bulky and hazardous process and when performed by human operators there is always a margin of error. However, robots are capable of repeatedly performing the spot weld operation in a reduced time with a negligible margin of error.

Aside from welding, robots also do assembling, spray painting, heavy lifting and the crash testing operations on the car. Robots today even install windshields on the car body. The automobile industry is constantly introducing new robots in their production facilities to improve the production of cars.

Robotics research is now focused on a new breed of intelligent robots with improved vision systems, intelligent sensors and sophisticated algorithms capable of multitasking and effectively replacing human intelligence with Artificial Intelligence (AI). However, this new generation of robot remains largely a vision of the future. As Ranganath Misra of Fanuc robotics puts it, "I know of only one running in production in the U.S., and a few in the development labs. There might be a half dozen in Japan."

The application of intelligent robotics currently can be found in Nissan's Intelligent Body Assembly System (IBAS), employed in the automobile framing station at the Smyrna, Tennessee facility. IBAS is a programmable flexible retooling auto body jig that can be reconfigured using simple computer software manipulations to assemble 30 different car types. IBAS effectively replaced the massive precision setting jigs that were used to hold the different car parts together during welding. Since each car part has different dimensions, jigs of different dimensions were needed to hold different car parts. With IBAS, a single automated jig can be effectively retooled to hold different body shells for retooling. The IBAS is in effect a combined robotic system, where 35 part handling robots hold together a vehicle's floor, body sides, roof and other major components of the shell to an accuracy of +/- 0.1 millimeter, while 16 other welding robots attach the parts together in 62 spot welds.

At the core of the IBAS is the Numerical Control (NC) locator, which controls the actions of the robots according to the car body type. As the car body leaves the IBAS, the NC locator uses touch sensors and laser rangers to measure all critical dimensions. If the locator finds any car part out of the specification, it can compensate the changes by adjusting numerical values. Moreover, the IBAS works by producing a graphic simulation in the computer, so any potential adjustment problems can be worked out before the exact assembly. The IBAS line is capable of completing one car in about 45 seconds, thus creating a monthly capacity of 20,000 units. The IBAS system is a clear example of how industrial robots are extensively used in the automobile industry to replace human labor. The fascinating speed, accuracy and efficiency of an IBAS system cannot be in any ways matched by manual labor.

Some other robotic systems currently employed in the automotive industry include the following:

KUKA KR 500 Robot: A 6-axis robot with a 500 kg payload, the KR 500 is floor mounted and has a large work envelope. The robot has a robotic mass of 2350 kg and an H reach of 2836 mm.

Fanuc S-430iW Robot: This is another 6 axis robot with a 165 kg payload. It is a heavy-duty floor mounted robot with an H reach of 2643 mm. Its slim arm and wrist make the various parts accessible to the robot and its fast speed ensures higher cycle time. The robot uses a Fanuc servo drive system, thus resulting in fast point-to-point positioning.

ABB IRB 6620: This is the lightest robot in its category. It can also work bending backwards and thereby has a considerable downward working area.

Recently, ABB introduced the IRB 5500 robot at the China Industry International Fair 2010, targeting the Chinese automotive industry. This new robot reduces its cycle time by 20% and paint consumption by 12 % from the earlier IRB models under certain specified conditions. The new robot is capable of an acceleration of up to 24m/s2 and painting speed up to 1.5-2 m/s. The IRB 5500 has a robotic arm which is able to move parallel both on vertical and horizontal car surfaces, thus ensuring a higher quality painting process. ABB claims that two IRB 5500 robots can complete the task previously done by four robots.

Other Industries That Use Robots

So called "clean room robots" are used in the electronics and semiconductor industries. The incorporation of clean room robots in the semiconductor industry results in major cost savings by reducing scraps from broken wafers and chips. Apart from machine loading and unloading, the other uses that the semiconductor industry robots are put to include parts transfer, product assembly and packaging.

Robots are also widely used in the construction industry for a variety of purposes. Robots are generally used in the construction industry to replace human labor in dangerous situations. Human labor still forms the crust of construction industry because the application of robots in the construction industry is still more expensive than human labor. In this industry, robots have been designed for applications such as inner pipe crawling, excavation, prefabrication and reinforcement.

In the aircraft and the aerospace industry, robots are used for functions like robotic coating systems (airframe, fuselage and component) and robotic water jet coating systems.

Limitations and Disadvantages of Industrial Robots

Apart from the obvious disadvantage of massive unemployment due to application of industrial robots, there are certain other limitations to industrial robots. For instance, the robots still lack eye-hand coordination to a large extent and they cannot match human dexterity. A robotic hand, however developed, still does not match the efficiency of a human hand. The robots are bulky apparati that demand considerable installation cost apart from the cost of buying the robot. Moreover, as robotic technology is developing very fast, companies may be required to install new models frequently to stay competitive. The payload to robot weight ratio in industrial robots is poor, often less than 5%. Adding new tools or effectors to a robot might require considerable reconfiguration of the robot and sometimes the new tools may not be compatible with the existing robot model. Robots are also occasionally prone to mechanical failures and erratic behavior that can lead to industrial accidents.

Robot Safety

A significant problem associated with industrial robots is the issue of occupational safety. Robots have been the cause of some major industrial accidents, so proper precautions must be maintained while handling these sophisticated and bulky machines.

Although industrial robots are used to replace humans in hazardous work conditions, they can be the reasons for industrial accidents, too. The types of accidents that have been caused by industrial robots have included impact or collision accidents, crushing or trapping accidents and accidents caused by mechanical failures of robotic components. Accidents may also arise from laser beams shooting from the robots, or from the welding sparks arising from a robot. The sources of these hazards have been human errors, unauthorized access to the robot's working envelope, accidents caused by improper installation of the robots, power system failure and environmental sources like the electromagnetic or radio frequency interference. However, the industry has been on a continuous learning curve from these early accidents and continuous research has been devoted to making robots safer.

Industrial Robots and Unemployment

Industrial robots can perform a wide range of functions and as research and development continues, they are increasingly able to perform more tasks. Obviously, the more tasks that robots can perform, the less jobs there will be for human workers. Between competition between domestic and overseas manufacturers and the effects of the recession, US manufacturing companies have little choice but to follow the trend towards increasing their employment of robots and decreasing the employment of human laborers. This increased demand leads in turn to increased research and development of robotic applications and lower prices for them.

In addition, nations are increasingly employing the use of robots because of the prestige associated with them. A nation who is a leader in cutting edge technology has a distinct advantage over a less advantaged country. Currently, the United States and Japan are the biggest players in this competition, but China, Korea and some European manufacturers are quickly catching up. The theory seems to be that the greater the use of robotics in a nation's manufacturing sector, the more prestigious and influential the country will be.

While the development and deployment of robots since the 1960s has been erratic, it has also been relentless. Now that trade unions no longer have their former power and influence, there is nothing to prevent the further expansion of the use of robots in manufacturing. The effects of this in the automobile industry are already evident. Other, newer industries, such as advanced electronics, have a shorter history of labor to look back on, but it can be assumed that robotics and related automated techniques prevented any large scale need for manufacturing employment from their inception. In the event that a new type of large-scale industry arises, it is likely that production will be primarily designed around robotic workers rather than human workers. In other words, even if the United States were to become the world's largest manufacturer of robots, US corporations would use more robots to manufacture the new breeds of robots.

Manufacturers of robots counter this argument by saying that their industry creates jobs. The Robotics Industries Association (RIA) argues that the use of robots in automation prohibiting outsourcing of manufacturing work to overseas economies like China, Mexico and India, thereby adding to the US GDP. RIA also argues that manufacturing robots still needs human labor, so the expansion of the robotic industry is actually creating new jobs. The RIA presently represents some 225 robot manufacturers, so there is definitely scope for new jobs in the manufacturing, supervision, maintenance and sales of the robotic units, but far more jobs are being lost to robots than are being created by their manufacturers.

Is light manufacturing and exception to this rule? While the emphasis of this presentation has been on the use of robots in large scale manufacturing, there is plenty of evidence to suggest that even smaller manufacturing concerns are increasingly turning to automated systems, if not in all cases strictly robotic systems. In many small and medium sized kitchen manufacturers, for example, the kitchen designer sits down at his computer and, after designing his kitchen, sends an order out to an automated saw that precisely cuts boards to their required lengths and widths. Depending on the size of the manufacturer and his budget, many more automated features can be added, such as edging, drilling and even many aspects of cabinet construction. Furniture manufacturers routinely use duplicating machines for carving and shaping. These are all jobs that were once performed only by skilled craftsmen.

Automation does not stop with the manufacture of an item, either. Increasingly, robots and other automated equipment are being used in the warehousing and other sectors for the same reasons they are being used in the manufacturing sector - because they are faster, more efficient and, increasingly, cheaper than human labor.

There really is no solution to the employment crisis in the manufacturing sector. If laws were enacted to outlaw or limit the use of robots in the manufacturing of automobiles in America, the automobile industry, already on life support, would collapse due to competition from other countries. If high duties were imposed on foreign manufactured goods, nobody would be able to afford to buy them. This is the dilemma those who are concerned about the future of employment for the average working class citizen face. Coupled with corporate America's zeal in adopting new technologies and its desire to eliminate costly and inefficient human labor, the most likely outcome is going to be a complete meltdown of jobs in the manufacturing sector of the US and overseas economies.

2
Falling Dominoes:
Retail America in Crisis

According to the National Bureau of Economic Research (NEBR), the current recession began in December of 2007. They made the recession official one year later, in December, 2008, based on data collected throughout the preceding months. Between January of 2008 and November of the same year, over 1.2 million jobs were lost in the United States. Those job losses began in December of 2007, hence that month marked the beginning. Other events, such as the collapse of Lehman Brothers, were just further, more dramatic signs of the trouble America was in.

At the close of 2010, 3 years has passed and America is still in recession. We have had several recessions since the close of WWII and snapped back from them, making the post war Baby Boom years the most prosperous years in the nation's history. However, only the most starry-eyed optimists believe that we will come out of this one unscathed. For one thing, the longest any previous recession lasted was 16 months. By December 2010, the "Great Recession" had already lasted over 36 months, with no real signs of change for the better. For another thing, this recession has cost Americans far more jobs than previous recessions and although the pumping of billions of dollars back into the economy has added a few encouraging statistics to the job rosters, nobody is really excited about the "recovery." In fact, any objective reading of the situation suggests that even though the national mood is anything but buoyant, Americans are in denial about the severity of the situation.

While the focus of the media has been and continues to be on government bailouts both here and abroad, the biggest reason why the retail trade and the American workforce can't expect a return to the "good old days" anytime soon is staring us right in the face - literally. Since its meteoric rise from the ashes of the NASDAQ bubble burst on March 01, 2000, the internet has come to dominate every facet of our lives. What began as the "Information Age" has gone on to become the "eCommerce Age" - it's the way we do business and do our shopping.

As consumers become accustomed to making purchases online, they move inexorably from purchasing MP3s, videos and books to buying clothes, household appliances and household furnishings online. Each consumer who makes the transition from buying his goods at retail outlets represents another lost customer to retailers.

How We Got Here

America is known as the "consumer society." The phenomenal growth of so called "emerging economies" like Brazil, India and China is due largely to the voracious appetite of the American consumer and our purchasing power. A couple of events are largely responsible for the phenomenon of the Baby Boomers and, ultimately, for the quagmire we're in today.

In 1966, history was made when the first purpose-built container ship sailed from Port Elizabeth, New York to the Netherlands port of Rotterdam. Within 10 years, millions of containers were being shipped from and to virtually every port in the world. The rise of the Chinese export economy can be directly traced to this era. The flood of cheap goods from China and elsewhere into the United States led to the development of the giant shopping malls that have become such a ubiquitous presence in America.

If we are a nation of consumers, how can we afford to consume so much? Prior to 1971, we were on the gold standard. What this meant was that every dollar bill was backed by gold. In 1971, President Nixon took us off of the gold standard. The result was an increase in credit and an increase in purchasing power. We became a nation of borrowers. This was fine as long as housing prices and the stock market continued their relentless rise. We could afford to buy on credit because our homes were paying the bill and our stock market portfolios remained healthy. That's no longer the case and it's not likely to change in the future. Now America is in the horrible position of being both in debt and, increasingly, out of work. With less money to spend, fewer goods are purchased and the shopping malls of America wait in vain for customers.

So far, retail giant Wal-Mart is one of the few "brick and mortar" retail companies that has remained unfazed by the economic downturn, largely because whatever sales it has lost from lower income consumers have been made up for in purchases from middle income customers looking for cheaper bargains.

Even Wal-Mart is facing an increasing threat, though. This threat comes in the form of online retail giants like Amazon and eBay. As Americans look for more ways to save money and these gargantuan internet enterprises find ways to deliver more goods faster and more economically, online shopping is increasingly becoming an American way of life. Wal-Mart is facing this threat by aggressively and innovatively utilizing IT systems through its website presence and Point of Sale (PoS) hi-tech strategies.

While giants like Wal-Mart are successfully making the transition to the internet, many other retailers are falling by the wayside. Those that are limiting their internet exposure or considering it to be a minor part of their operations are failing as the world turns away from traditional retail outlets to online virtual stores.

The first sign of things to come came when Napster created the first music sharing program. Had the recording industry not successfully shut down Napster's free music swapping site, the industry may have collapsed. More recently, Napster's successor, Limewire, has been ordered to shut down for copyright violations. While these measures may save the recording industry as a whole, services like Apples iTunes are taking a large chunk of potential sales from retail record outlets.

Video stores are facing a similar fate with the increasing popularity of Video on Demand services from telecommunications giants like Comcast, Time Warner, Netflix and now Amazon, the world's largest online retailer. While it is understandable that digital products like software, music and videos would pose a threat to retailers across America, what about tangible goods, like clothing and appliances?

The Death of the Shopping Mall

A visit to your mall can tell you more about the decline in retail sales more than all the statistics in the world. A recent article in the Wall Street Journal, *Recession Turns Malls Into Ghost Towns,* says it all. While the 2009 article emphasized the recession, changing demographics and the general trend away from malls to Wal-Mart, it also mentioned that "In the 12 months ended March 31, U.S. malls collectively posted a 6.5% decline in tenants' same-store sales." In other words, the decline was universal, regardless of location.

The death of the shopping mall is such a noticeable phenomenon that there are even blogs and websites devoted to the subject. A blog on Mediaite.com titled *How the Aughts Killed America's Malls and Newspapers* makes a point the Wall Street Journal missed:

"The blossoming of the Internet in the Aughts, a time of political and economic instability, has hastened (though not completed) the demise of many cultural components tangential to its core functionality. The slow sublimation of newspapers is understood to be its victim; the evaporation of malls, America's once dominant retail touchstones, is not. Both industries are sliding down similar slopes, pushed by the same hand."

That hand is the internet. While the demise of the traditional newspaper can be directly traced to the internet, the shopping mall is facing attacks from several directions. Whether the recession, changing consumer preferences or the internet deals the death blow is a moot point. Every vacated business in a shopping mall represents a loss of jobs. When shopping mall giants like the ironically named General Growth Properties, which owns 200 malls across America, files for bankruptcy and when Standard & Poor's lowers the credit rating of the entire department store sector, it is a given that tens of thousands of jobs will be lost in the fallout. How many jobs? According to the United States Bureau of Labor Statistics, in the month of November, 2010 alone, 28,000 jobs were lost in the retail sector. 9000 of these were in department stores and 5000 were in furniture and home furnishings stores.

November was not an isolated month, either, but it is a significant one. November is traditionally the month when retailers are gearing up for increased Christmas sales. It is the month when temporary staff should be added, not removed from the workforce.

At least some of those 28,000 retail workers will find employment. Those who live in the Lexington, South Carolina area may be able to find work in the new Amazon warehouse that is being built there. According to the Charlotte Observer, the new warehouse is going to be finished in time for the 2011 Christmas season. Amazon will be looking for 1,200 permanent new staff and expected to hire up to a further 2,500 temporary staff to handle its anticipated Christmas orders.

What the GDP Tells Us

In GDP statistics, "General Merchandise" is roughly the equivalent to the range of department store merchandise, while "Non Store Retailers" include both electronic (internet) and mail order sales. A comparison between sales statistics for these two sectors gives a fairly accurate picture of where our dollars are being spent. For example, a comparison between the census data for the years 2001 and 2008, the latest year for which statistics are available, yielded these results. The numbers are in millions of dollars:

2001: General Merchandise: 527,887
2001: Non Store Retailers (electronic and mail order): 114,844
2008: General Merchandise: 596,935
2008: Non Store Retailers (electronic and mail order): 227,084

Overall, general merchandise sales increased modestly, by approximately 10%. At the same time, non-store retail sales *nearly doubled*. These increased "electronic and mail order" sales represent a large bite out of department store and other general merchandise "brick and mortar" store sales and although no statistics are available, it is more than likely that mail order sales have been in steady decline over the years, as even rural and semi-rural consumers are now making their purchases online. In fact, Spiegel, the mail order catalog giant, now has an online catalog in addition to its printed catalog, as do its rivals Sears, Roebuck & Co. and Montgomery Ward. Not to have an online catalog today would be suicidal.

Amazon

With book sales topping 5 billion dollars in 2009, Amazon became the largest bookseller in the world, followed by Barnes and Noble, whose sales reached over 4 billion dollars, a decline of 5% on the previous year. Borders Books had sales of $2.6 billion, which was down 15% on the previous year. Significantly, while Barnes and Noble store sales were down, its online subsidiary, BN.com earned modest revenues of $573 million dollars in 2009 - up from $466 million in 2008. Furthermore, in July 2010, Amazon sold 180 digital "Kindle" books for every 100 hard cover sold. If any statistics reveal the trend away from buying in retail outlets to buying online, these do.

Still, books are a niche market and the trend towards digital books helps explain the public shift away from retail outlets to online book buying. Is there any real indication that Americans are also buying their clothes, appliances and other household goods online? Amazon's sales of general merchandise are significantly up over previous years, but what about their online competitors?

The Top Ten Internet Giants

It is common knowledge that Amazon is the world's largest online shopping center. While much of Amazon's early success can be attributed to its entry into book sales and digital products, all of the other Top Ten Internet Giants sell tangible goods and have had to fight for internet recognition. Unlike Amazon, their online operations are also in competition with their own retail outlets.

Below is the list of the Top Ten ecommerce sites as compiled by the industry watchdog, Internet Retailer. According to the same source, Amazon takes a huge 19.4% slice of the internet sales pie, but the other 80% is taken by office supply merchants like Staples and Office Depot and mass merchants like Wal-Mart, Sears and Best Buy:

1. Amazon (mass merchant)
2. Staples (office supplies)
3. Dell (computers, electronics)
4. Apple (computers, electronics)
5. Office Depot (office supplies)
6. Wal-Mart (mass merchant)
7. Office Max (office supplies)
8. Sears Holdings Inc (mass merchant)
9. CDW Corp (computers, electronics)
10. Best Buy (computers, electronics)

These are the companies that are changing the purchasing habits of the American public. Unlike Amazon, they are companies that achieved their initial success through traditional retail models, but saw the writing on the wall early enough to cash in on the internet revolution. Meanwhile, those retailers who continue to cling to the notion that business in the malls and shopping centers of America will pick up as soon as the recovery takes hold are finding themselves with a lot more free time than revenues on their hands.

The Relentless Growth of eCommerce

While the shopping malls of America continue to die a painful death, ecommerce goes from strength to strength. Internet Retailer reported some interesting statistics in May, 2010. While the sales figures for ecommerce sites looked modest, with total sales amounting to $134 billion as compared to total retail sales of just over $2 trillion, ecommerce's sales amounted to a 2% increase over the previous year, while retail sales as a whole fell by 3%. That 5% differential is not an isolated or temporary state of affairs, either. It is an ongoing trend. It is also noteworthy that the growth in ecommerce has occurred during the deepest recession since the Great Depression.

The article went on to quote Nikki Baird, a partner in RSR Research: "People still have to shop for necessities and last year the web was the bargain hunter's best friend. Even if they just shopped for the basics, consumers still did more of their buying over the web."

Also interesting were the numbers regarding internet sales by the large retail chains. Out of the top 50 store chains, 26 of them enjoyed online sales growth, while their retail outlets experienced a decline in sales. Of the rest, 11 either had faster internet growth or a slower decline in sales than their retail stores experienced.

These are the sales statistics for retailers who are effectively competing with themselves. Online, all of them are competing with Amazon, who began as an online merchant and since its inception has focused all of its energy on perfecting the ecommerce business model.

The Amazon Phenomenon

From a business perspective, Amazon is the model every online retailer seeks to emulate. In 2009, Amazon grew 14 times faster than the rest of the ecommerce market. This was not simply because of its high visibility or Kindle sales. Amazon consistently makes customer service its goal and seeks to overcome the one advantage retail outlets have over online sales: delivery time. In October 2009, they began offering same day delivery service in New York and 6 other major metropolitan U.S. cities. Since ordering a product from Amazon on a mobile device can be done in a matter of seconds and you can have it delivered to your door in almost the same amount of time and with far less effort than it takes to drive to a shopping center, it's no wonder that in the 4th quarter of 2009, Amazon's revenues greatly exceeded analysts' expectations when they reached $5.45 billion dollars - an increase of 27% over the previous year. 43% of that revenue came from "Sales of electronics and other general merchandise."

What About the Other Guys?

Amazon is the king of ecommerce. It's understandable that they would have a significant impact on retail sales across the country and around the world. But what about the other retail chains - the ones that while large and influential, do not have the online clout of Amazon?

Macy's is not a minor name in retail merchants, but like other department stores throughout the country, the recession posed a challenge to them. They answered the challenge by increasing their investments in their "dot com infrastructure" and away from their stores. This is understandable, since their total revenue declined by 5.6% while their internet revenues have grown to an estimated $1.24 billion.

Macy's is not an isolated example. The same thing is happening with the Gap, Saks, Toys 'R' Us and dozens of other of the largest and most prestigious retail chains in America.

What About the Other eCommerce only Sites?

Aside from the large retailers with recognizable names, who are using their established names to their advantage online, there are hundreds of specialty sites that have no past retail history whatsoever. These are the sites that started as online businesses and don't have the baggage of retail outlets to carry. Are they making a significant dent in the retail sector? Take a start-up ebusiness that specializes in diapers, for example. Surely, when you need diapers for your baby, you would just pick them up on your way home from work, wouldn't you? Apparently not.

Diapers.com is a newcomer to ecommerce. It launched in 2005 and made two and a half million dollars its first year. That's impressive enough, but in 2009, it made Internet Retailer's Top 100, taking the 85th spot. In that year, its revenues grew to $182 million dollars, up from $89 million the previous year. That figure represents millions of diapers purchased online and not from corner stores, pharmacies and grocery stores. Not resting on its laurels, the company is expanding into baby clothing, car seats and strollers. Aside from savvy internet marketing, Diaper.com attributes its growth to its free overnight shipping to two-thirds of the continental U.S.

Boutique ecommerce success stories like that of Diapers.com are not isolated flukes, either. Of course, for every ecommerce start-up that succeeds, 99% or more fail, but that has always been true in business. The numbers of start-up ecommerce sites is in the millions. Many of these are just individuals looking for their niche in the vast internet marketplace, while tens of thousands of others are start-ups like Diaper.com with capital and expertise behind them. While the numbers are not available, just a look around the shopping centers and downtown shopping districts of the United States will tell you that nobody's starting up a new chain of general merchandise stores. If all the money is going into online enterprise and not into brick and mortar retail outlets, clearly there's not much hope for a resurgence in traditional retail trade.

The eBay Behemoth

Collectively, one of the biggest threats to retail America is the customer, who, thanks to eBay, has become both a seller and a buyer at one online location. Back in 1995, Pierre Omidyar started eBay in his living room in San Jose, California. His aim was to produce an auction site where sellers could set an opening price and sell for the highest bid. It was an instant success, attracting tens of thousands of sellers and buyers. This number quickly grew into the millions and eBay set its sights even higher.

From eBay's perspective, the problem with having millions of people selling odds and ends online is that the profits per sale are minimal. eBay answered the challenge by attracting more upscale sellers with name brands to sell. While millions of individuals take small nibbles out of the retail market like a school of piranhas, these larger companies are like sharks, swallowing retailers whole.

As impressive as the growth of ecommerce has become, it still accounts for only 7% of total retail sales in America. Combined with the recession, that 7% has already sounded the death knell for thousands of retailers, but it's not enough for eBay. They recently acquired Jack Abraham's start-up, Milo.com for a rumored sum of $75 million. Milo.com is an inventory search engine. Abraham's original idea was to create a better online product comparison website. His theory was that there are some products that people still prefer to buy in retail stores. They like to try on clothes, for instance. Increasingly, they go online first, to find the best deals, but they end up going into the store to make their purchases.

Now that Milo.com has been acquired by eBay, you can still use it as a comparative shopping website and are encouraged to do so, but while you're at it, eBay scours its database looking for the best deals on your product and related products that you can buy from them. While you may still make your purchase in the store, eBay becomes your starting point and price point.

It gets even more interesting, because eBay has a smart mobile app called RedLaser, which you can use in-store to take photos of bar codes and find better deals elsewhere. Meanwhile, eBay is collecting data about your purchasing preferences and, like the Google ads you get on the sidebar of your email that just seem to know the kinds of products you are likely to buy, eBay will send you notices about deals on eBay you might be interested in.

The whole thrust of the venture is to change people's purchasing habits. The habit of going into a physical store to make a purchase is deeply engrained in consumers; but it is just a habit. Once eBay has implanted itself in the consumer's mind as the shopper's friend, they will think *online* instead of *in store* whenever they shop for anything. It's just a matter of time before they make their purchases on their mobile devices during their lunch break rather than waste time going to the shopping center.

The Brave New World of Warehousing and Sales

Is there a ray of light in America's hopes for an improvement in the job market - retail or otherwise? After all, some sources, such as Logistics Today, take a more buoyant view of the future of business in the U.S., expecting a growth not only in production but in profit margins. However, the same source enthuses about the improved logistics in the manufacturing and warehousing sectors. For example, Wal-Mart boasts that they intend to expand their use of RFID (Radio Frequency Identification) technology in order to increase efficiency. RFID is well known to consumers: this is the technology that makes bar code scanners possible. Now that all business can be "wired" to the internet, a simple swipe of a bar code can do much more than give sales staff the price of a product: it can send that data immediately throughout the chain of supply and tally orders automatically. Increasingly, this even filters down to the warehouses and manufacturers. In the future, according to Bill Hardgrave, head of the University of Arkansas' RFID Research Center (which incidentally is partially funded by Wal-Mart):

"We are going to see contactless checkouts with mobile phones or kiosks, and we will see new ways to interact, such as being able to find out whether other sizes and colors are available while trying something on in a dressing room. That is where the magic is going to happen. But that's all years away."

"Contactless checkouts" means no sales personnel when translated into plain English.

PepsiCo, the snack food and beverage giant, is improving efficiency by utilizing Direct Store Delivery (DSD) systems, which eliminate the need for a tiered warehousing and delivery system. Wikipedia's definition of DSD includes these words: "bypassing any retailer or wholesaler logistics." How is this accomplished? According to the same article, by the use of a computer language called Standard Interchange Language (SIL). In simple terms, this computer language allows a variety of different software applications to "understand" one another, enabling them to work as an integrated unit.

"Bypassing any retailer or wholesaler logistics" can roughly be translated as "cutting out the middle man" - the "middle man" being thousands of administrative, clerical and other staff.

These are just two examples of how logistical improvements come at a cost to the American workforce. As long as we remain in the digital age (and if for some reason we were "unplugged," the situation would be unimaginably worse) there is not a great deal to look forward to in the retail sales or materials handling job markets. The internet reaches through all sectors, improving efficiency and eliminating the need for the most inefficient link in the supply chain: the human worker.

Just In Time (JIT) Inventory Management or lean manufacturing is a system of inventory management designed to eliminate waste in the production and distribution of goods. This begins at a manufacturing plant in China or Malaysia and continues right down the supply chain through to a warehouse distribution center in Des Moines. In essence, JIT analyzes every facet of an operation and seeks to eliminate waste by reducing costs and increasing efficiency.

The concept of JIT is not really a new one. Henry Ford adopted it in the production of automobiles. The difference today is that the internet and technology has made it possible to streamline the process enormously. In order for JIT to work, the entire supply line has to work as a single unit. Because inventories are kept at an absolute minimum, yet must be sufficient to keep up with demand, order processing becomes a constantly fluctuating process. A manufacturer of small parts in one part of the world must be informed on a virtually daily basis at the same time an assembly plant elsewhere is kept abreast of orders. It is a highly complex process and is dependent on an unbroken stream of communications throughout the supply chain. These communications are made possible by the internet.

Dell Computers is an example of JIT. Dell takes orders directly from customers at both the wholesale and retail level and only manufactures computers on demand. In the rapidly changing world of computer technology, this has resulted in the company being able to deliver the latest advances in computers faster than its competitors, improve customer relations and virtually eliminate excess inventory and materials handling. Dell is able to keep an inventory of only five days - far ahead of any of its competitors, whose inventories must be as much as 20 to 30 days ahead of anticipated sales. As a result of employing JIT, Dell has now become the market leader in computer sales.

JIT II

In 1986, Bose implemented JIT II, a concept that virtually makes the customer an employer. Other companies have followed suit and are doing so increasingly in order to meet the challenges of the recession. As David Marble, Vice President of JITII development for United Printing Inc. a Rhode Island based company says: "Stronger supplier alliances allow for more control over budgets and headcount. The benefits for the supplier include increased volume and the opportunity to expand the range of products offered."

Note the word "headcount" - employees. "Contactless

Checkouts", "bypassing logistics" and "headcount" are all different ways of saying the same thing. Nobody likes to say it directly, but the key to increasing efficiency while at the same time reducing costs is in reducing the number of workers. In the manufacturing and warehouse sectors, administrative staff is reduced by software applications and the internet, while production workers are being eliminated by computer based and even internet connected robots. The Point of Sale (PoS) is increasingly a computer or mobile phone screen, not a checkout clerk and, when RFID technology is perfected, those customers who wish to try on their clothes before they buy them won't have to deal with sales staff, either.

Robotics

Robotics sales, hit hard at the outset of the recession, is now enjoying a growth spurt as companies seek ways to trim production and materials handling costs. An article on Robots. com enthuses about the advantages of Pick and Place robots. These robots are "among the most popular material handling systems." They have advantages over their human counterparts in virtually every way. As the article says: "Work cells create more because they perform applications with more accuracy, speed and tirelessness" (sic). Note the truncated sentence: "more accuracy, speed and tirelessness" than what? Obviously, the answer is, "than their human counterparts."

Other material handling procedures robots can do today include dispensing, palletizing (loading and offloading pallets), packaging, order picking and many more jobs that currently require human workers. Bear in mind that these are jobs that robots can do today and the industry is really still in its infancy. It's not farfetched at all to envision a day in the near future when an item swiped through a "contactless" RFID checkout in Des Moines will connect directly to a pick and place robot in a South Carolina warehouse, which will then load the item along with others onto a pallet, which will in turn be taken by an automated forklift and placed onto a truck which hopefully will be driven by a human driver back to the retail outlet in Des Moines. Of course, if the product is purchased online, the driver can deliver the product directly to the customer's door, eliminating the need for any retail outlet or staff whatsoever.

The Delivery Process

The small business owner who is clinging to the hope that his store has a future because he doesn't have to charge a freight fee is tragically behind the times. Between the internet's ability to streamline order processing and the increasing volume of goods that are being purchased online, transportation costs are now very low. They are so low; they dwarf the cost of leasing a store and paying staff.

If someone buys a bottle of perfume in a department store, the cost of leasing the store space, paying staff and all of the other overheads associated with running the business have to be factored into its retail purchase price. Most of these overheads are eliminated with online stores. They do, however, have to factor in shipping costs. How, then, can Amazon, eBay or indeed even someone who sells handmade soap she makes in her back yard afford to offer free delivery?

In a word, the answer is "logistics." As outlined above, the internet has made it possible to all but eliminate the human element in warehousing, inventory management and even sales. A smaller internet marketer has access to the same services and facilities that Amazon or eBay uses. When his site attracts an order for a bottle of perfume, the order is processed electronically from the moment the customer leaves the online checkout to the moment the product arrives at his door. The order goes directly to the appropriate warehouse, which electronically processes it. Either robotically or through human order pickers, the perfume is taken from the shelf, packaged and loaded onto a pallet along with hundreds or thousands of other individual products going to the same destination. All of the logistical complexities are taken care of online.

UPS, the delivery giant, knows more about logistics than perhaps any other company in the world. On their website, they call their approach to logistics "The New Logistics." In their words:

"The new logistics lets you operate with the heft of a big guy, no matter what size you actually are. You can design a product, get a prototype made, and have it land on your desk in just days. Sell products to customers in Bangalore--right out of your basement."

This is not just sales talk. Thanks to their "massive integrated network of physical, technological, and human assets," UPS is able to deliver on their promises. They are not the only delivery service in the world that can do this, but they are the largest and, arguably, the best. For the customer, whether it's the guy shipping to Bangalore out of his basement or a multi-national corporation, the interface between UPS and the customer is its deceptively easy to use website. Orders can be placed, tracked and paid for without dealing with a single customer service representative. While UPS does have over four thousand retail UPS stores throughout the United States, it also has nearly 40,000 drop boxes, eliminating the need for more retail outlets to physically handle the goods.

When a UPS client places an order for a delivery online, he immediately becomes an integrated part of the entire system. UPS connects directly with his own computer's order entry system. In this way, it is as if the client is a data entry employee of UPS whose only job is to place and track his own orders. This makes the whole procedure seamless, saving order processing time and money. Every other order processing point is similarly electronically connected, allowing the customer to track his own orders, whether they are in a warehouse, aboard a container vessel or on a delivery truck bound for their destination.

It is online delivery systems like UPS's that make it possible for Diaper.com and tens of thousands of other ecommerce sites to be able to offer free same day or overnight delivery. This is just one more reason why retail stores in America and elsewhere are facing such a crisis.

The Big Picture

The upside of the United State's enormous buying power throughout the second half of the 20th century was the amount of capital that was available for developing new technologies. Without venture capital and cheap loans, the IT giants like Microsoft could never have gotten off the ground and without borrowing money to purchase PCs and laptops, Americans would not have embraced the internet with such fervor. Other nations have lagged behind the U.S. in acquiring the technology, but today, the fruits of all that development are available in every corner of the globe. It doesn't require more than a rudimentary understanding of English to set up an English language ecommerce site. A small shop in Kathmandu can sell Tibetan singing bowls to customers in England, Australia, the United States or any other country where English is spoken. An eco-lodge in Cambodia's Cardamom Mountains can tell the world where to find them. On a micro-scale, the internet represents opportunity to millions of small businesses throughout the world.

On a larger scale, Alibaba, the Chinese ecommerce giant, reported that its third quarter profits for 2010 were up 55% from the previous year. Alibaba, who counts Wal-Mart and Procter and Gamble among its customers, operates from three separate platforms. While they are best known in the West as a trade platform for wholesale exporters and importers, they also have platforms for domestic trade within China as well as a Japanese platform. In all, Alibaba has 56 million customers in 240 regions throughout the world and are expanding rapidly. In 2010, the company sought to extend its reach in the United States with the acquisition of Vendio and Auctiva and launched customer service operations in India.

A customer success story on alibaba.com demonstrates just how effectively this Chinese wholesaler is helping ecommerce erode the American retail sector. Online Sales, Inc., a Pennsylvania based ecommerce business saw an increasing market for American flags in the wake of 9/11 and began business as an online shop for patriotic Americans wanting to buy flags. Owner Kevin Hickey turned to Alibaba to find overseas manufacturers for his flags. As he says:

"Alibaba.com has helped us grow by enabling us to purchase high-quality low-cost products from abroad with little or no research costs, like overseas visits, phone calls, agents, etc."

As a result of the internet's efficiency, Online Sales expanded its product range and grew from a million dollar business in 2002 to a

25 million dollar in 2009. Tellingly, this company was able to deliver at a time when the retail sector failed. The Swine Flu outbreak in 2009 caught retail merchants unawares and they rapidly ran out of protective face masks. Within a week, Online Sales had 250,000 face masks ready for online sale and sold them all. The result was a quick $40,000 profit for them and a similar loss for retailers in Swine Flu affected areas in the United States.

When asked if he had any tips for doing business in a recession, Hickey quipped: "What recession? Our sales are up 20 percent and we are making more money than ever." For online merchants like Online Sales there may not be a recession, but for the American retailer, the "Great Recession" is looking more like a Depression every day. This phenomenon is not limited to the United States, either - or at least not for long. The internet knows no boundaries and has no patriotic loyalties. Alibaba helped Kevin Hickey find cheap overseas suppliers of American flags. Patriotic American consumers purchased them online in droves in the wake of 9/11. Alibaba's newest venture, Alibaba Express allows international retail customers to buy online at near wholesale prices. For instance, you can purchase an "original blackberry (sic)" made in Hungary with an Arabic keyboard at Alibaba Express. Yes, free shipping is included in the purchase price.

Much of the global expansion of ecommerce goes under the radar of the American public, whose focus is on the recession and the dwindling hope that the nightmare will soon be over. While politicians argue over whether or not the latest stimulus plan is going to work, the internet marches forward. While shopping mall owners and tenants put their heads together trying to figure out ways to attract customers back into their doors, the internet marches forward. The only retail merchants who are surviving the recession are those who are closing their doors and logging on. This is not a passing fad. It is the future. Sure, a few merchants whose overheads are low, like the little shop in Kathmandu that sells Tibetan singing bowls, won't need to close up shop, but any retail business whose overheads are high and profit margins low is virtually doomed. At some time in the near future, this will be as true for retail businesses in China, who are currently enjoying an annual growth rate of 18%, as it is in America.

Is there a solution to the problem? Is there a problem at all or is it just a change that's taking place? It's certainly a problem for the tens of thousands of retailers who are trying to survive and their millions of employees, but it doesn't look like there's a solution, short of outlawing ecommerce - and that's no solution at all. The fact is, the "good old days" are gone for good. The retail merchants of America and the world are falling like dominoes. It's a matter of survival now and the only way to survive is to be selling online.

3

Realtors Redundant in Wake of the Internet Revolution

Real estate and the American Dream have always had an intimate connection. Indeed, the attraction of America for many of the first settlers was the opportunity to have their own piece of land to cultivate or exploit as they saw fit. As the country grew, things got a little more complicated. Land had increasing monetary value and the complexities of buying and selling property eventually led to the establishment of a new profession: the Real Estate Professional. Real Estate brokers, the business owners who were legally entitled to handle the complexities of the sale, were at the top of the heap, while their assistants, the Real Estate agents, handled much of the sales work in exchange for a slice of the commission.

In the post WWII era, real estate as an investment took off. Instead of paying a down payment on a home and working hard to pay off their mortgages, the new generation of Americans saw their home as an opportunity to prosper. They bought "fixer uppers" in desirable neighborhoods and sold them at a profit. Those with the means or borrowing power to do so built whole new suburbs on large swathes of empty land and sold them at a profit. Of course, this had been going on since the first brownstone was built in New York City, but the trend reached a frantic pace as the 20th century came to a close. "Flipping" houses was the only smart way to invest in real estate when you could buy a home for almost no money down and realize a profit almost before you had to start making the repayments.

Right up until the bubble burst in 2007, realtors were cashing in on the American Dream. After the bubble burst, both realtors and their clients were the first to suffer and they suffered the worst. Overnight, hundreds of thousands of real estate salesmen and women found themselves sitting behind their desks, wondering what to do with the rest of their lives. With no commissions, they had no livelihood and their employers, the brokers, let them go in an effort to survive the crisis.

How many were laid off? It's not an easy question to answer because the big real estate brokers, like CB Richard Ellis, were hesitant to say. However, according to a 2009 article in the *Wall Street Journal, Real Estate Pros Go Moonlighting*, employees in real estate offices fell 17% between 2007 and August of 2009. This number did not include real estate agents, most of whom are self employed. In states worst hit by the recession, the numbers were even higher. In Florida, for instance, 29% of employees in real estate offices lost their jobs.

Another interesting statistic cited in the article was the decline in incomes of real estate professionals. The median income of real estate agents nationwide fell from a 2004 high of over $49,000 to just $36,700 in 2009. In the hardest hit areas, incomes dropped 50% or more and everywhere, formerly prosperous realtors were forced to "moonlight" in jobs they formerly felt paid too little to support their lifestyles, but now were the only sources of income they could find.

What the *Wall Street Journal* didn't mention was the internet's effect on jobs in real estate. That is probably because, as is true in so many other sectors of the economy, the effects of the recession were so dramatic. The internet, on the other hand has been encroaching on real estate more stealthily. According to the National Association of Realtors (NAR), in 2010, 91% of American homes were sold by real estate agents; the other 9% being private sales. However, the NAR also notes that 97% of home buyers used the internet to search for homes. If they use the internet to search for homes, why don't they as yet use the internet to bypass brokers and agents and buy direct? In increasing numbers, they do, but a shell shocked community turned first to the traditional real estate company in the wake of the recession.

Prior to the recession, real estate brokers and agents looked at their online presence as a largely promotional tool. In the vast majority of cases, if a homeowner wanted to sell a house or someone wanted to buy one, they would contact a real estate agent in their area and let them handle the details. It was actually easier than buying or selling property online because the agent did everything for them and in a booming market, their commissions were deemed affordable. Post-recession, though, when the value of a person's property often falls well below the amount they owed their lending institution, a five or six percent commission is a crushing added expense. The extra effort needed to sell direct is increasingly seen as not just one option, but the only viable option.

There is increasing evidence that real estate agents can no longer cling to the hope that their industry will rebound even if the market picks up. In an effort to save money, home sellers are turning to online Multiple Listing Services (MLS) and For Sale by Owners (FSBO) platforms to sell their homes. An MLS charges a flat fee in exchange for a listing, while FSBO sites use a variety of other income streams to make a profit. In the statistical data, MLS sales are lumped in with real estate agent sales, but critics argue that for all intents and purposes, MLS sellers are also private sellers. MLS sales now comprise 10% of all home sales, so it can be argued that up to 20% of all real estate sales are now private sales. Since so many of these sales are initiated and largely conducted online, the argument that the internet has not been responsible for job losses in real estate loses credibility.

Foreclosures and Short Sales

While America waits with bated breath for an economic recovery and financial pundits focus on every ray of light on the economic horizon, the housing market continues its relentless decline. Many optimistic observers who confidently stated the market bottomed out at the end of 2009 were strangely quiet when 2010 statistics showed that sales were down nearly 26% in October 2010 from the previous year. The real estate industries "salvation," if that is what it can be called came in the form of foreclosures, which accounted for 34% of home sales in the United States in October, 2010, up from 30% in October of 2009. Foreclosures are bank sales and are handled by real estate brokers on behalf of the banks.

Another area where some real estate agents are continuing to profit is in "short sales." A short sale is an alternative to foreclosure in which a homeowner agrees with a bank to sell their home at a small loss rather than have to go into arrears or unsustainable debt. Short sales are relatively complex transactions that banks insist be handled by experienced realtors.

Neither foreclosures nor short sales give real estate agents the big commissions they want, but they do keep a handful of them afloat. How long they remain their "bread and butter" no one can say, but if they were hoping for a recovery last year, almost no one is anymore. A January 12, 2011 Foreclosure Fraud blog bears the title, *Housing Market Slips into Depression Territory*. Without wasting time or words, the article begins with this: "Home prices have fallen 26 per cent since their peak in June 2006, worse than the 25.9 percent decline during the Depression years".

For Sale By Owner Sites

Homeowners don't need to be told that the housing industry is in "depression territory." Millions of those who managed to escape foreclosure are taking proactive steps to minimize their losses while they still can. They are advertising their houses online using For Sale By Owner (FSBO) platforms. Sites like ForSaleByOwner.com offer buyers and sellers all the tools they need to skip the middle man and legally and safely conduct real estate transactions between individual parties. Aside from a few hundred dollars paid to an attorney to help with the legalities, there are no other fees or commissions to worry about. Compared to real estate commissions that can make the difference between a profit or a loss in today's market, the cost is negligible. On its FAQ page for sellers, ForSaleByOwner.com bluntly asks the seller to: " Calculate 6-7% of what you think your house is worth, then ask yourself: is it worth paying this much to have someone else show my property". On its FAQ page for buyers, the site points out that the agent's commission is usually tacked onto the selling price and that buying a home from a private party is actually easier than buying through a middleman (the realtor), who will be acting on his own behalf.

FSBO.com, another one of America's leading private property sale websites, reports that the average amount of money saved by selling a property directly through their website, rather than using a real estate agent, is $8,002. Those who wish to use their Multiple Lising Service (MLS) are assured that they, too, can "save thousands of dollars" in reduced commissions.

Flat Fee MLS

Those who do not wish to sell their properties themselves are finding Multiple Listing Services to be a cost saving alternative to going directly through their local real estate agent. In the case of an MLS, the seller enters into a 'limited services agreement' with a realtor who lists their property for sale in the local Multiple Listing Service (MLS). This is generally done for a set fee.

There are two important distinctions between a 'flat fee MLS' listing and a 'full service' listing:

* The flat fee agent is normally acting in a limited capacity on behalf of the seller
* Fees are normally paid up front, rather than commission being paid at closing based on the sales price of the property

The aim of 'flat fee MLS' is to reduce the cost of selling a property to the individual. Instead of offering all their full range of services, a real estate agent simply pays for the online MLS listing. The seller retains much of the responsibility for selling the property including arranging 'open houses' and other marketing. While 'flat fee MLS' won't eliminate a real estate agent's fees (a buyer's broker commission of 2-3% is still generally payable), it does save sellers a significant amount of money.

Even the National Association of Realtors, whose website attracts over 5 million visitors per month, is pushing MLS. Through their site, users can contact realtors across the country directly and make MLS arrangements with them online, without ever having to meet them in person. The NAR may be doing this to save its own skin, since, according to the *Dallas Fort Worth Real Estate News* membership in the National Association of Realtors has decreased by around 300,000 since the property market's peak. The article goes on to say: "Over the last four years, the number of licensed real estate agents and brokers has declined by approximately 25% while the number of transactions has declined by a faster pace.... Gross commissions have also declined by about 50% since the start of the decline."

As buyers, sellers and realtors struggle to find light at the end of the real estate tunnel, they all are increasingly looking to the internet for their answers. As they become comfortable with the various platforms offered online, the internet becomes the natural place to conduct business. After saving thousands of dollars in commissions online, what seller is going to return to a traditional real estate agency? After cutting back on staff and in the process saving hundreds of thousands of dollars, what broker is going to pull the plug on the internet, even if the market recovers? The jobs lost in the real estate sector are gone forever and there are more to follow.

Real Estate Brokers and Agents Are Worried

According to Cnet news, real estate brokers and agents were already worried about the effect the internet was going to have on their bottom line back in 2006, before the bubble burst. A July 28, 2006 Cnet article, *Real estate's Net turf wars*, covered a San Francisco real estate conference devoted to the subject of selling real estate online. At least one of the speakers, David Liniger, founder and chairman of major real estate agency Re/Max International seemed to be in denial about the effect the internet was going to have on his business. The internet 'has not put us out of business," he said, "It will not put us out of business." Steve Ozonian, CEO of Help-U-Sell, an online franchise company that charges flat fees instead of percentage of sale value commissions, disagreed, stating that the "real estate industry needs to realize that the genie is out of the bottle."

While David Liniger can still say that Re/Max as a whole is not yet "out of business," its largest Florida office is. Re/Max headquarters declined to comment when inews published the news that *Florida's Biggest REMAX Office is Shutting Down* on August 12, 2010. The article pointed out that in addition to the obvious slow down in business caused by the recession, the reason behind the closure of what had been a Fort Lauderdale institution for over twenty years was that "Realtors simply have not learned how to utilize technology."

Real estate brokers have tried to compete by improving their own online presence and stressing the complexity of the house buying process and the need for an expert to be involved. However, when weighed against the cost and convenience of FSBO websites, these advantages look pretty weak. And when mainstream news shows like the CBS Morning Show give viewers *The Basics of Online Real Estate Sales* and say, "These days it's not a luxury to use the Web to buy or sell a house, it's a necessity," those out-of-date realty companies that cling to their old business models are dooming themselves to redundancy. While the segment doesn't go so far as to suggest ditching Real Estate agencies altogether, it does caution viewers who are not internet savvy to get their "teenaged nephews" to help them put their "best online foot forward."

This is an important point and one that is overlooked by those like David Liniger who think the internet is not a threat to their business. The next generation of home buyers, those who are going to be taking advantage of all the foreclosures and short sales, are internet savvy. The internet is their preferred method of communicating and doing business. "Brick and mortar" businesses are as outdated as the horse and buggy to them. While those homeowners who are not as "internet savvy" are turning to FSBO and MLS websites out of desperation, the new generation will skip the middle man altogether and go to the FSBO sites only. There will be no place at all for real estate brokers and agents in the near future except perhaps to help the elderly who don't have "teenaged nephews" buy and sell their homes.

The Mortgage Finance Industry:

The mortgage finance industry, which was largely responsible for both the real estate boom and bust, is suffering the same fate as the real estate industry. Hundreds of thousands of employees, including receptionists, processors, sales agents, marketing staff and secretaries have lost their jobs and the internet is making sure their jobs will not be coming back. MSN Money reported in 2007 that 40,000 jobs were lost in the mortgage industry in the first eight months of 2007 alone. According to the Mortgage Employment Index as reported by the *Latest Business News* website, fewer than half of the 535,400 people who were employed in the mortgage industry in October of 2005 remain.

In addition, it is not just the stagnant nature of the housing market that is resulting in mortgage industry redundancies. In the same way that FSBO sites are leading to dwindling numbers of real estate agents, mortgage websites are replacing traditional mortgage brokers.

It is easier than ever to head online and research the mortgage deals that are available. Borrowers can search the web and find a deal they like. All they then have to do is to fill out an online form and the system can automatically make a decision about whether the borrower qualifies for the loan. Instant credit scoring and credit searching can be done online meaning that borrowers no longer need to seek the advice of a mortgage broker.

As more and more people head online to find the mortgage finance they need to buy their property, more and more people employed in the traditional mortgage industry will lose their jobs. This, combined with the enormous job losses since the beginning of the recession, is going to ensure that this once vital business sector will never again be a source of employment for anything approaching the numbers it employed in the past.

The Bottom Line

The bottom line in the real estate industry is that the global recession just accelerated a trend that was already beginning to occur. Cutting costs and improving efficiency are two goals in any industry. Any industry that can find a way to cut back on labor costs will do so. The internet is the ideal vehicle for selling real estate. Why would a real estate broker share his commission with an agent if he didn't have to? By taking advantage of the internet, he can spend much more time in the office and less out in the field. Instead of needing a half dozen agents to help him with his workload, one or two will more than suffice, even in a busy office. Of course, his office isn't going to be very busy anyway, since his customers are going to be going to FSBO sites. If he is clever, a broker who works through an online Multiple Listing Service will pick up some small commissions that way, but not enough to pay for his office expenses. Many brokers have already closed up shop and gone home to work online and many more will continue to do so in the future.

As in so many other sectors of the economy, the internet is proving to be a curse to the real estate and related professions. Brokers and agents alike are joining the unemployment lines. The "lucky" ones are finding work elsewhere, but, like the former Coldwell Banker sales manager who was laid off from his $75,000 plus real estate job and found a $35,000 a year job in law enforcement, they aren't likely to being enjoying the lifestyle they once enjoyed, especially since they still have their own mortgages to pay off on homes they cannot sell. Perhaps they'll be able to unload them through a FSBO website. One thing is for sure: they won't be going to their neighborhood real estate agent. It's just not worth the cost and hassle, when you can so cheaply and easily do it yourself online, even if you do need to enlist the help of your internet savvy "teenaged nephew."

4
The Crash Landing
of the Travel Agent Industry

The travel industry in the United States was one of the first industries to become computerized and also one of the first to embrace the internet as a booking, sales and marketing tool. Throughout its history, the travel industry has been embroiled in controversy as airline companies competed against one another and even against the travel agencies who have traditionally served as intermediaries between the carriers and their customers. In recent years, it has been an ongoing battle for travel agencies and as consumers increasingly use the internet to make all of their travel arrangements, it is a battle that travel agents across the country have already lost. Those few that survive are like wounded soldiers who still wear the uniform, but no longer engage in active combat.

In order to gain insight into how travel agencies, who might otherwise have been in a position to capitalize on the internet, found themselves struggling for market share in the gargantuan global travel industry, it is necessary to take a look at the history of the industry as a whole. The airline industry took full flight in the postwar era, when a prosperous nation began traveling by air both domestically and internationally. Throughout the 1960s and most of the '70s, the airline industry was strictly regulated in the United States by the Civil Aeronautics Board (CAB). CAB regulations included everything from the routing of aircraft to setting the retail prices of flights. While the intention of these regulations was to ensure efficiency and fairness in the marketplace, it did not encourage competition.

In 1978, President Jimmy Carter appointed Alfred Kahn, a strong advocate of deregulation, as head of the CAB. As a result, the airline industry was one of the first large public industries to be deregulated when Kahn successfully pushed the Airlines Deregulation Act of 1978 through Congress. With their new, unfettered freedom to compete and conduct business largely without government oversight, the major airlines began jockeying for market share. While the carriers argue otherwise, saying that deregulation led to cheaper fares and better service for consumers, Consumer Reports and other consumer advocate groups argue that fares actually increased over the ensuing decades compared with what regulated fares would have been and service became poorer. At the same time, in order to increase profits, the major airline carriers took steps to reduce commissions to travel agents and used the emerging computer technology to engage in unfair and sometimes illegal competition.

The Role of the Travel Agency

Independent travel agencies were initially welcomed by the airline carriers as intermediaries between them and the consumer. The travel agent was the one who had face-to-face contact with the customer and made all of their travel arrangements for them. This was synchronous with the development of the Computerized Reservation System (CRS), an outgrowth of the earlier Airline Reservation System (ARS). Deregulation accelerated the growth of computerization and the Global Distribution System or GDS was a further evolution of CRS. These systems proved to be so efficient they remained virtually unchanged until the internet era. Collectively, all CRS/GDS systems are often referred to as CRS systems.

In the years after deregulation, travel agents comprised a vital link in the supply chain that connected the providers with consumers. The agents, via CRS/GDS, handled seat reservations and processed payments via the credit card companies. In addition, they handled hotel reservations, car rentals and other details for clients. In exchange, they received commissions for their services. In the case of the airline companies, travel agents originally received a 10% commission on seat reservations. While in theory this was an efficient, cooperative system, in practice it was anything but.

Development of the GDS

The history of computerized flight reservations began in late

1950s when American Airlines decided to develop an Airline Reservation System to allow real time access to the complete flight details of American Airlines at all its offices, so that the booking process would be integrated and automated. This led to the launch of Sabre (Semi Automated Business Research Environment) by American in 1964. The launch of Sabre was one of the earliest feats of computing and it led to the ability to price seats on an airplane according to different well categorized levels. Sabre was the first ARS in the market and other carriers soon followed with their own proprietary ARSs. Sabre belonged to the AMR Corporation, owner of American Airlines.

In 1974, Robert Crandall, an executive at American Airlines, proposed that all airline companies jointly own a computerized communications network that they would share with travel agencies. In this way, they could prevent travel agents, who were very powerful at the time, from taking control of the reservations systems. The other airlines balked at the suggestion and instead of devising a single ARS, developed separate systems

In 1976, United Airlines began the process of installing their own in house Apollo CRS in travel agencies. American soon followed with Sabre. The airlines now began handling direct calls from travel agents, acting as a representative of the traveler, and then cataloguing these calls in their own computerized systems. The ARS and the CRS concept worked well for the companies, making automation an even more favorable option. In the late 1980s, Apollo's annual pre tax return on investment had reached 70 percent, while that of Sabre was more than 100 percent. By 1987, two consortia were formed with the European Systems Amadeus and Galileo, operating on the same principles as their US counterparts (Apollo and Sabre).

However, since the CRSs were owned by airline operators, fair competition practices were violated. New carriers voiced complaints of excessive fees and in the fight for screen position bias manipulated fare displays and searches. The need for legal restrictions became evident and Congress launched an investigation in 1982 to confirm the presence of screen position bias and other unfair practices. This further led to the establishing of a comprehensive set of regulations in 1984, which were reissued again in 1992.

Meanwhile, the CRSs developed in to GDS by mid 1990s. Travel agents used GDS to check and confirm flight schedules, issue tickets and make hotel bookings. GDS operators collaborated with travel service providers, including airline companies, cruise operators, hotels, railway companies and car rental companies. The travel agents were now empowered to not only make hotel and flight bookings, but also arrange for special meal requests and perform back-office allocation jobs for the consumers. Thanks to proprietary GDS systems, travel agents were an indispensable link in the supply chain, while the owners of the systems, the airline carriers, maintained control over their computerized systems and continued to be able to employ strategies to manipulate ticket reservations in their favor.

From GDS to Internet Bookings

The internet entered the travel market in mid 1990s. The adoption of internet booking systems was partially driven by market pressure to end the rampant corruption of CRS/GDS systems. Also, GDS provided the required framework the internet needed, thus vastly lessening development time. However, there were major loopholes in the regulations designed to prevent corruption. For instance, the regulations permitted secondary display bias under certain circumstances and the difference between primary display bias and secondary display bias was not defined adequately. These corrupt practices therefore went on uninhibited with the key players fighting over the major share of profit.

Carriers were constantly manipulating flight schedules to let their flights appear at the top, thus depriving consumers of more cost effective travel options. If a carrier was being penalized for an elapsed time algorithm tied to connections over a congested airport, it simply changed the connecting time or flight time to improve its listing positions. This practice was nicknamed "time shaving." Carriers even sometimes invented new algorithms to facilitate screen position bias in flight listings. In addition, the CRS rules in the US were not applicable to European providers and exorbitant fees began to be charged from providers. To make matters worse, the interrelations between the travel agents and service providers were not always cordial as both aimed to carve separate profit niches, letting the other suffer losses. This continued bias in computer reservation systems led a major section of providers to seek alternate ways of business transaction and the internet provided them with the opportunity.

The arrival of the internet quickly became popular with consumers because it gave them greater power. The key players recognized this and soon established internet presences to adapt with the changing times. For instance, AMR Corporation launched its travel website Travelocity in 1996. The Microsoft Network (MSN) launched the travel website, Expedia in 1996. Expedia was later sold by Microsoft to USA Interactive (Interactive Corp).

The Beginning of the End for Travel Agents

The internet affected all components of the supply chain. From providers to credit card companies (and the travel agents), everyone had to made accommodation in the new rules of game set by the internet. The combined force of the travel business had to give in to the demand of increased consumer participation made possible by the internet. In addition, the key operators of the business saw the opportunity to cut distribution costs by bypassing the intermediaries and approaching the consumers directly. This led to increased acceptance of the internet in the industry.

In addition to Travelocity and Expedia, other travel related websites began to emerge. Travel agencies, hotels, car rental companies, airlines and tourist organizations all jumped on the internet bandwagon. Competition drove these websites to vie for consumer attention and develop 'consumer friendly' user interfaces. Some travel websites like PC travel, Preview Travel and Worldview did not manage to survive in the changed conditions and vanished from the market. Others, like Travelocity and Preview Travel survived and prospered by merging.

The biggest change was undoubtedly increased customer participation in the system of travel booking. The links of the supply chains slowly began to break and the travel agencies were the first to suffer as airline carriers chose to approach consumers directly, as did other travel providers. Airlines, in fact, categorized travel agents into two groups; online and traditional and created different compensation scales for each group. Between 1996 and 2001, the number of traditional travel agents reduced by 15%. A 'pay for performance' payment system soon got established and many travel agencies struggled to survive in the changed business environment. Those who did survive did so by changing their focus from the traditional brick and mortar business model to the digital model. Many invested in electronic servicing capabilities and offered to act as online representatives. Travel agents became incorporated into the corporate travel arena by offering services like back-office processing, information management and on-site passport processing.

Travel Agencies Redefined by the Internet

The problem for traditional travel agencies was that if they wanted to survive, they had to become *virtual* travel agents and focus their energies and budgets on developing their online presence rather than on opening and staffing new outlets in shopping centers. This costs jobs. According to Career Overview, a career search engine, those seeking careers as travel agents increasingly need advanced college degrees "due in large part to the ease of travel booking on the internet." The article goes on to say: "As more information is available on the internet and as telecommunications advance, more travel agents work at home."

The Bureau of Labor Statistics agrees. In a 2009 report, they stated that the "ease of Internet use and the ready availability of travel and airline Web sites that allow people to research and plan their own trips, make their own reservations, and purchase their own tickets will result in less demand for travel agents for routine travel arrangements."

The internet has redefined the travel agent. Ask a search engine to find "travel agencies" for you today and sites like Expedia will dominate the listings. Other, more traditional agencies such as STA Travel are also listed, but when you go to their homepage, instead of being offered a search facility for offices in your area, you are given search facilities for booking online. STA does have a "Find a Store" tab, but the company has only 18 brick and mortar outlets throughout the entire United States. All of these are located in major metropolitan cities, primarily on the East and West coasts.

Clearly, travel agencies are undergoing a metamorphosis. Today, the very expression has already become out of date. When people want to find travel professionals, they look for travel *sites* rather than travel *agents*.

Types of Travel Sites

Internet travel sites can be basically categorized into three categories. These are travel service providers (branded sites), destination sites and virtual branches of traditional brick and mortar travel agencies.

The major online travel sites like Travelocity are *branded sites* that are developed and operated by major airlines to promote the airlines. They do not direct the consumer to lower fares on other airlines, so the consumer must do comparison shopping on other sites to get a correct estimate of the average price range and find lower fares. These sites also offer hotel bookings and transportation facilities with other companies with whom they collaborate.

The *destination sites* offer information about particular destinations. Most destination sites usually represent regional or national tourism boards of various localities. The primary goal of destination sites is to promote visits to favored destinations and give information about the attractions of a particular destination, so they are often less concerned with the mechanics of how to get there.

Virtual branches of travel agencies provide comparative airfares (including cheap current deals), offer hotel reviews, giving trip planning advice and sell travel-related merchandise

Internet Travel Industry Business Models

The internet travel industry follows four types of business models. These different models may work alone or in combination with one another. The different business models of an internet travel industry include:

The merchant model: These sites bring buyers and sellers together on a common platform. Key market players who sell their goods and services via their websites typically operate such sites. Expedia and Travelocity are in this category.

The advertising model: These sites provide valuable travel information and at the same time generate revenue from the adverts placed on their sites.

The review model: Such sites review the different destinations and are designed to provide valuable travel tips to the travelers. The reviews also help the travelers make the best hotel and transportation arrangements.

The community model: These are community websites maintained by travelers. The travelers themselves post their views and reviews of a place and share important travel tips with fellow travelers. Virtualtourist.com is an example of such type of site.

How Travel Sites Are Set Up

A typical travel site is divided into different categories such flights, hotels, car rentals, vacation packages, cruises, maps, business travel and travel deals. Travelocity, Expedia and Orbitz were among the first sites that entered the online market. Orbitz shareholders include American, Continental, Delta, Northwest and United Airlines, according to a 2002 report. These remain the key players in the travel market today. Travel sites offer search facilities on their sites so that the travelers can sort through the different travel options and decide for themselves the best mode of online travel. For instance, Orbitz has incorporated ITA search software with its Google based search engine to make the travel search easier and uncomplicated. It is this same ITA software that Google purchased in 2010 to make it the preferred site for travel searches, leading to wide speculation about the survival of the travel agent industry. Besides Orbitz, other prominent players using ITA software for their travel searches are Kayak.,Microsoft Bing and Trip Advisor. These are not always amicable relationships, a fact demonstrated recently by TripAdvisor when it blocked Google Places from accessing its online travel reviews.

Another key player in the arena is the Sabre Group or the Sabre Holdings. The Sabre Group still holds a prime position in the travel industry. Sabre Holdings offers retail merchandising of travel related products and services and provides distribution and technology solutions for the travel industry. The Sabre Group operates through four separate companies, with Travelocity being the largest. The Sabre Travel Network is the travel agency arm of the group, providing solutions for the travel industry. Sabre Airlines Solution caters to the airline transportation industry. Finally, there is the Sabre Hospitality Solution for the hospitality industry.

With the development of the Online Travel Industry (OTA), the demand for low prices has remained a persistent one. Websites such as Priceline and Hotwire allow the user to bid for tickets and hotels to enable consumers get a lower price deal on travel services. Both these websites also have regular search features that let you see the fares without bidding. However, the catch here is that you won't know the carrier airline, departure time or actual hotel until you have booked the ticket. Only those travelers with flexible schedules find such websites helpful. The average Christmas time booking fare as recorded by Priceline in 2010, stands at $422, as compared to $431 last year Christmas. These sites divide their services into different categories like airfares, hotels, rental cars, vacations, tours & attractions and cruises.

Some other sites like Kayak and Vayama offer vertical search engine services to travelers, allowing them to browse through different price and schedule listings. Vayama is a part of the third largest travel company in the world, BCD Holdings NV. Vayama offers deals from ALL airlines and ALL airfares, including overseas low cost carriers. Over 400 airlines are listed in Vayama. Farecast.com, the MS Bing travel network site, provides an airfare forecast, gives users an estimate of the general airfare range and notifies users when fares drop.

Travel review integrator sites like Trip Advisor and Yahoo! Travel provide reviews of hotels and airlines to assist the traveler in the travel choices. TripAdvisor offers reviews on flights, cruises, hotels and restaurants. The site hosts more than 40 million different travel reviews. TripAdvisor operates through a conglomeration of travel sites covering all aspects of travel. The family of TripAdvisor sites include VirtualTourist, SmarterTravel, TravelPod, Bookingbuddy, airfarewatchdog, onetime.com, Seatguru, Cruisecritic, Family vacation critic, Independenttraveller and Flipkey. As noted above, TripAdvisor recently blocked Google places from accessing its reviews. The reasons of this blocking varies from technical difficulties to the affiliation of TripAdvisor to the FairSearch campaign group, which is against the Google acquisition of the ITA software.

These are just a few of the many travel sites that are available online. Others include online versions of the popular travel guidebooks like Frommer, Fodor and Lonely Planet. Then there are the specialty travel websites, such as TripHub, which categorizes travel destinations and offers in terms of general interests such as golfing, skiing, weddings and spas.

These "virtual travel agents" have far greater scope and can offer travelers far more information than any independent travel agent possibly could. When you can simply type "backpackers hostels in New Zealand" into any search engine bar and be instantly directed to a site like Hostelworld, which offers reviews of backpacker accommodations throughout the world, why would any internet savvy member of Generation X or Y bother to go to a travel agent, who in all likelihood would do exactly that and then try to sell you a ticket through his preferred airline carrier?

Increasingly, travel agents are being used only by older travelers who are not familiar with using the internet and corporations who use them for corporate travel needs. These are small segments of the traveling community and a relative handful of travel agencies can fill these niches. Even internet newbies who are unsure about how to make online travel arrangements or how to get the best deals can go online and get all the information they need on independent blogs and forums. Needless to say, a travel agent is not going to be forthcoming with such information, because it would cost him the job he is so precariously clinging to.

Gadgets and the Travel Industry

Mobile devices like cell phones and smartphones are making it easier than ever for people to make their travel arrangements online, providing travelers with the means to make their travel plans anytime, from anywhere. With the global reach of the internet and a mobile device equipped with the right travel apps, it is no longer necessary to make all of your travel arrangements before you travel. There is an app for virtually any travel need. Aside from allowing you to book transportation, finding a hotel in a strange city is as easy as browsing on your smartphone. Built-in GPS devices give precise directions to anyplace you want to go. If you wish to travel by train, there are apps available for getting train schedules and fares. With all the convenience they offer, it is little wonder that a 2003 survey by Yesawich, Pepperdine & Brown discovered that 80% of business travelers took their cell phones with them while another 20% carried Pocket Digital Assistant (PDA) devices. In 2003, mobile device apps were in their infancy. Today, they are at the cutting edge of internet technology. Taking a mobile phone and a laptop on business trips and even vacations is a virtual necessity in the second decade of the 21st century.

The following list of some currently available travel apps gives a fair idea of why there is simply no need to seek the services of a travel agent anymore:

TripIt: This free app tracks airline miles and sends alerts to its users whenever there is a flight delay. The app helps you prepare a complete travel itinerary and sharing the itinerary with anyone whom you want to share through your mobile phone or your computer.

GateGuru: This Free app offers a gate by gate layout of the airport where you are traveling. The app is available for most US and Canadian airports.

HopStop: Hopstop is a free app that guides travelers through the public transport system of 16 cities across Europe and US. The cities included in HopStop include Paris, New York, San Francisco and many other major cities. Simply enter your start and end points to find connecting public transport links between those places.

Yelp: Yelp is a free app that helps travelers find restaurants and other places to visit while you travel. You can search places by ZIP codes or city names by this app.

Google offers three essential apps for travelers. These are the currency converter, the driving guide and the translation tool.

Facebook travel apps are among the most popular. Some of these apps include the Hostelbook.com app that is used to find backpackers hostels throughout the world. Not only can you find the hostels and read reviews about them, you can make your reservations through this app. For travelers looking for hotels, the Hotelme Facebook app from Kukunu.com provides similar information to the Hostelbook. com app.

The travel apps market on mobile phones is one that is still underused. New research by analytics firm Complete shows that only 38% of Smartphone users conduct travel research on their Smartphone and 28% use the phone to book flights or hotel rooms. The survey also shows that only one fifth of the total Smartphone users have installed travel apps on their device. This is undoubtedly going to change in the near future as the use of mobile devices for purchasing products has only begun to capture the public imagination. Nonetheless, those 28% of users who do use their mobile devices to book flights and hotel rooms represent millions of people who in the past would have relied on travel agents to help them do these things.

Social Media and the Travel Industry

In 2008, guitarist Dave Carroll of the band Sons of Maxwell had his guitar broken by the mishandling of United Airlines staff. After repeated customer grievance calls that were of no avail, the musician made a YouTube video, "United Breaks Guitars." This was his way of expressing his grievances. The videos became a viral sensation and had a huge negative impact on United Airlines. In just ten days, approximately 4 million people viewed the video. It earned a place in CNN reviews and even received full articles in leading newspapers like USA Today, the Los Angeles Times and the Sydney Morning Herald. As a result, United Airlines stocks plummeted 10% and the company lost $180 million dollars.

This story illustrates the power of social media and the impact it can have. Without YouTube and the other social media sites, customer grievances could not be aired. With them, customers can reach an audience of millions and have an affect on the future of a company. This incident did not go unnoticed by other airline service providers and has actually had a positive effect on their levels of customer service. The story also illustrates that consumers increasingly turn to their fellow consumers online for advice about everything, including the airline company they choose, rather than rely on authority figures, who are viewed with skepticism at best. The travel agent is one such authority figure.

Another such authority figure is the airline company itself. The internet has made it possible for the average person to gain access to information the airline companies and big travel websites would rather they not have access to. The same bias that the airline careers created in their CSR applications is being used online, but in a different way. As far back as 2000, *Consumer Reports* discovered evidence of bias in supposedly objective travel sites. Even many sites that are not owned by an airline company or consortium of airliners accept advertising fees from these companies and give them priority listings. For example, the study revealed that on Travelocity, advertised airlines were given dominant flight listings. On Lowestfare, TWA flights with less than ideal itineraries were nonetheless rated first. Cheap Tickets, Expedia, Lowestfare and Travelocity all failed to list various airlines at all, even though they had viable route itineraries.

This information and the conclusions of other studies have been publicly available since the year 2000 and are continually updated. Such mistrust of both the airline companies and the supposedly unbiased travel websites opened the door for the only internet "Superpower," Google, to make a play for absolute domination of the online travel industry.

Google ITA Software Acquisition

ITA Software was founded in 1996 by a team of MIT computer scientists, around the same time as travel websites were emerging on the internet and it has been one of the components that have shaped the online travel industry. ITA's QPX software enables the customizing of travel data and is used by major travel companies as the travel search tool on their sites. ITA allows users to customize their travel searches and receive refined search results based on a wide number of parameters.

On July 10, 2010, Google announced that it had reached an agreement to purchase ITA Software for $700 million. In its Press Release, Google argues convincingly that by employing the software directly into its search facility, it will benefit everybody. The short video clip attached to the PR shows how it will improve searches by listing airfares, flight times, carriers and all other relevant data directly in its search results rather than just listing the top listings according to Google's current search algorithms. Since these algorithms rate results according to other factors than relevance, the ITA program should theoretically give consumers more objective and relevant data.

Google argues that since it is not a travel agency, its purchase of ITA Software will not have a negative impact on competing online travel companies. Furthermore, the company argues that because Google does not currently use a competing software program, it will not affect market share of similar programs.

The real threat of Google's acquisition of ITA Software is to existing travel sites. For this reason, industry leaders like Expedia, Travelocity and Kayak have joined together to form a group dubbed Fairsearch.org. The threat posed by Google in its acquisition of ITA is what prompted TripAdvisor to block Google's use of its travel reviews on Google Maps.

Google is not, however, without allies from within the travel industry. Orbitz and Priceline are two online travel giants who support the move and Arthur Frommer, founder of Frommer travel guides, has publicly stated that the "current situation [in airfare search] is untenable. It needs Google to straighten it out." An important wild card entrant at this debate is Southwest airlines. At present, they are active search engine marketers but they do not fully participate with OTAs with their flight data. The new Google-ITA deal is expected to bring Southwest to the forefront where its airfares will be compared with the key airlines.

The buyout of the ITA software comes at a point when the airlines industry has been going through a consolidation of its own, with United Airlines and Continental Airlines announcing plans to merge a few months ago. It is no secret that the airline companies are fighting for survival. Between fierce competition from overseas providers, the fluctuations in fuel prices and other factors, their survival is based on how much market share they can beg, borrow, buy or steal online. If Google robs them of the unfair advantage the larger airline companies now enjoy online, it could very well lead to the bankruptcy of many of the oldest and biggest names in the industry.

While the individual airline companies will undoubtedly go through tremendous changes in the coming years, consumer demand for airline seats remains as high as ever, in spite of the recession. The latest figures from the World Travel & Tourism Council show that the worldwide travel and tourism GDP is expected to rise by 2% this year, as opposed to an earlier forecast of 0.5%. Figures from the United Nations World Tourism Organization confirm the upward movement of the travel industry. The WTM also recognizes increased demand for value for money from consumers and their increasing reliance on social media sites such as Facebook. What is relevant to traditional travel agencies in these findings is the fact that consumer demand is increasingly sidestepping or completely ignoring them in favor of doing independent online research for the best travel deals.

Future Trends in the Travel Industry

Surprisingly, the recession did not have a debilitating impact on the travel industry. Although airlines had to combat the recession in terms of losing a major chunk of corporate passengers, the overall trend in the travel industry has not been discouraging. The participants at the World Travel Market (WTM) in November 2010, confirmed this. The WTM summit also confirmed cruising as a dominant travel trend in 2011, with 2010 recording a marked increase in cruise vacations.

Between the effects of the recession, fuel price spikes and fluctuations in currencies, the travel industry as a whole and the airline companies in particular are going to be facing increasing challenges in 2011 and beyond. According to industry insiders, the key focus will be to strike a balance between traffic and capacity. The strongest regions for air traffic will be the Asian markets and other emerging markets like that of South America.

Climate change and the impact of tourism on fragile ecosystems is also of concern to the travel industry. These matters were discussed at the December 2010 United Nations Climate Change Conference (COP 16) at Cancun in Mexico hosted an event, jointly organized by the UNWTO (United Nations World Tourism Organization) and the Ministry of Tourism of Mexico. Titled "Tourism's Response to Climate Change': What's Next?" the conference highlighted the fact that the objective of tourism should be to promote sustainable exploration of the world rather than thoughtless exploitation driven by revenues and profit. The event highlighted the importance of ecotourism and the importance of realizing the impact of the tourism industry on climate change. Mexico's minister of tourism Gloria Guevera pointed out that Mexico's marvelous natural beauty supports tourism activity, which in turn constitutes 9% of Mexico's GDP. Minister Guevera emphasized preserving this biological diversity for its own sake and for the sake of tourism. It was unanimously agreed that the tourism industry constitutes a major portion of the GDP in many countries.

A dominant future trend that is being recognized by everyone in the travel industry is the increased role that social media is going to play in deciding travel options. The industry is well aware that its future depends on better service at better prices and that both of these interests can best be served via the internet.

The Bottom Line

The bottom line is that tourism is not currently in decline and that the travel industry as a whole will continue to viciously compete for market share. In any competition, there will be winners and losers. Airline companies, cruise line companies and other transportation companies will change hands, merge and go broke, but they will not disappear. Hotel chains will go through shakeups, but there will always be a demand for travel accommodations. Vacationers will continue to rent cars, so there will always be a market for rental cars. Trains will crisscross continents, taking travelers to their destinations and cruise ships will sail the globe.

The only losers in the travel industry are the traditional travel agents. Once the indispensable intermediaries between consumers and travel service providers, their role is rapidly being supplanted by the internet. Those consumers who have not lost faith in their ability or willingness to give them the best prices simply see no need to make use of their services. The airline companies, who once relied on them to create the vital link between them and their customer base and were willing to compensate them for their efforts now actively seek to eliminate them from their supply chain, seeing travel agents as an unnecessary expense at a time when their survival depends on shaving costs wherever possible.

It is as if there is a dogfight in the skies and in cyberspace. While the future of many of the players is uncertain, travel agents lay wounded and dying on the battlegrounds below, abandoned even by their commanders, the travel agencies, who are agencies in name only, but in reality are unmanned online travel drones operated by computer software.

5

The Construction Industry in a Post-Recession, Digital World

With roots reaching back to when man emerged from the cave, the construction industry is one of the oldest in the world and certainly among the most influential. Today it remains an economic mainstay in countries across the globe, including the United States, where it made up at least $560 billion, or 4-5%, of the nation's $14+ trillion GDP—the market value of goods and services produced annually—in 2009. But, with unemployment rates at double the national average, the industry is in jeopardy. Economists say that, for construction workers, the recession has yet to end and there is none in sight.

Private demand continues at an all-time low as foreclosure towns grow and Internet commerce runs shopkeepers of all sizes out of business. Society is going mobile, changing how we live and work. Fewer families are planting roots, building homes, or even buying at all. The Internet is globalizing jobs, outsourcing certain positions to hubs around the world and slowly chipping away at office culture. The result is a surplus of property on the market and nearly a complete lack of demand for new homes or commercial spaces, which converts into fatal employment conditions for millions of construction workers and trades people. How did this happen? Will the construction industry survive?

The History of Construction

Before construction was a full-fledged industry, it was simply an act of survival. Early humans needed shelter from the elements and built basic structures out of stone, mud, wood and other natural resources they were able to find close to home. As humans divided labor responsibilities, people began to trade construction work for food, clothing, or other types of services, but the majority of early males still knew how to construct a typical dwelling.

At the dawn of civilization, when large stone structures became the first emblems of classic architecture, construction began to develop into an industry, though few volunteered for the job. Early construction work was grueling, to say the least and most laborers were slaves, many of whom were worked literally to death. Skilled laborers like stonemasons, on the other hand, were highly sought after and enjoyed an array of social perks after working their way up from apprenticeship.

Fast forward to the 18th century when the world was ripe for development, the population was expanding and technology was advancing at unprecedented rates. The construction industry was not far behind. The first winds of the Industrial Revolution began blowing across Europe with stone quarrying and advanced metalworking, inspiring a wide range of new architectural styles. In places like Britain, builders were eager to experiment with modern materials and urban zones soon exploded with new houses, shops, theaters and factories. Elements like slate, tile and brick had never been more in demand.

By the 19th century, the Industrial Revolution was in full swing, right in time for a growth spurt in the new world. Across the Americas, but concentrated in the United States, construction workers slowly pounded out the region's infrastructure—factories, mills, canals and railroads—and with it, erected a new, modern way of life. The construction industry reflected this change and in 1891, the first steel-framed building, or skyscraper, the Wainwright Building, was constructed in St. Louis. By the 1930s, elegant, towering buildings like the Wainwright graced cityscapes all over the world.

But just as buildings began to rise, the economy suffered a big fall with the Stock Market Crash of 1929. Wages were slashed, jobs were cut and new construction projects were either halted or delayed. Home buying fell with the economy as people pinched their pennies and waited for the depression to lift. When the recession rocked the economy in 2007, construction was similarly devastated. We're still waiting for it to bounce back.

The Construction Industry and the 2007 Recession

The last three decades leading up to the 2007 financial crisis were characterized by the steady growth of the GDP and people were spending and building with confidence. This is typical of a strong economy. Consumer spending generally reflects a country's economic index. When people are employed and forecasts are positive, new buildings break ground every day and existing structures undergo regular rehab while buyers indulge in more products and services, driving up demand. As demand goes up, business owners naturally ratchet up supply as well, investing in larger warehouses and office spaces to accommodate their increased product. And with a company's growth comes new employees to help manage its success.

But when an economy buckles, consumer spending plummets and the opposite happens. Reduced demand means fewer sales, making it hard for companies to pay for their warehouses and office spaces, not to mention their employees. As faltering businesses cut people from the payroll, it becomes more difficult for banks to collect mortgage payments and this leads to foreclosures so that banks aren't shouldering too many unpaid debts.

The 2007 recession didn't follow the last part of that formula. Relaxed, pre-2007 lending practices set up millions of homeowners to default on their mortgages should times get tough. After the housing bubble burst, those homeowners failed early on and were then forcefully vacated by the thousands, leaving ghost towns in their wake. Home values immediately plunged and those homeowners who managed to hold on faced drastic equity losses. All of that, combined with vast unemployment, has kept a glut of homes on the market with banks collecting nothing when they should be offsetting their debts.

It's a bleak scene—whole neighborhoods of houses sit empty in 317 of 337 metropolitan areas of the United States. As foreclosures send families fleeing, communities are falling into complete disrepair. In her report, "Nevada's story: Boom to bust in housing," Cristina Silva describes the situation in Clark County, Nevada. "Neighbors call to complain of abandoned houses, stagnant pools, wild yards and unsecured doors." In January of 2011, Nevada had the highest foreclosure rate in the nation.

Economists estimate that 2.1 million families will face foreclosure in 2011. If they are correct, by year's end, over 9 million families will have deserted their homes since 2007. And because when foreclosures hit a community, they quickly drain the remaining homes of value, few want to sell—or can. Millions of families are stuck in deteriorating communities because their homes are underwater. (Not surprisingly, along with sky high foreclosure rates, Nevada is also the underwater "capital" of the country.)

In a buyer's market, when no one is buying that means no one is building, either. When real estate went under and the economy went with it, the majority of private home building projects went by the wayside. In most places, investors have yet to pick up these, or any, projects again—a very bad omen because new construction is the single largest determining factor in whether the industry survives. Without new construction by private investors, there is no industry.

Construction in 2011

Today, while other industries slowly rebound, construction remains heavily depressed. Foreclosures and bankruptcies mean that homes and businesses lay vacant all over the country and few people are breaking new ground. Not an inch of the nation has been spared from the effects of the industry's sustained depression. In many places, construction of new homes, offices, apartment buildings, factories, schools and infrastructure has come to a complete standstill. And while there is plenty of work to be done improving, maintaining and repairing old structures, there is often a complete lack of resources to pay for it. Suppliers, contractors, plumbers and electricians, among others, are searching, usually without success. They few they find typically fall into one of three construction categories: buildings, heavy and civil engineering, or specialty trade.

Building construction makes up the majority of modern construction industry projects, encompassing all residential, commercial and industrial structures. Heavy and civil engineering construction refers to the building of roads, highways, tunnels, bridges, sewers, etc. Specialty trade construction is detail work like plumbing, electricity, carpentry and painting.

In the process of erecting or maintaining a structure, the construction industry necessarily intersects with a bevy of related industries, from architecture to landscaping. And because each project requires dozens of experts, trade specialists and professionals in order to finish, construction sites often seem like revolving doors with a steady stream of laborers that span the sector either coming or going. In peak economic times, this system means that construction and its related industries are fonts of employment. When hard times hit, construction is blighted by layoffs because of the diverse body of work performed by those in the vast industry: recently it has the highest unemployment rates in any segment of the economy.

Take a basic house construction project, for example. After an architect maps out a plan, the lumber supplier provides the contractor with building materials, which laborers will use to actually erect the new home. Once the house is up, an electrician will wire the building while a plumber puts in the pipes and drains. Depending on the location, HVAC professionals may be called in to install heating and air-conditioning systems. After that, painters, decorators and interior designers will then beautify the space, adding color, detail and decoration. In some cases, a landscape architect may design the outdoor space surrounding the home, completing the project with strategically placed flowers and foliage. That's a big team for a relatively small project. But when projects dwindle, how do the laborers, the craftsmen and the other professionals find work? The short answer is: they don't.

While the rest of the economy recovers, the construction industry is still wrestling with the effects of the 2007 meltdown; the most devastating consequence of which has been widespread unemployment. 21.8% of the industry is out of work. This is more than double the national average in all other sectors of the economy and, unlike other industries, there are no signs of a change for the better. The Associated General Contractors of America (AGC) released a study in early March of 2011 saying that construction employment continued to decline in 36 states from January 2010 to January 2011. Not only are laborers facing the worst job market since the Great Depression, but architects, suppliers, electricians, plumbers, HVAC professionals, painters, interior designers and landscape artists are finding themselves out of work, as well.

Economists don't predict a full recovery until private construction increases. But potential buyers and builders are terrified to invest in property or break new ground because they fear that the worst may be yet to come. In the meantime, construction workers and related professionals across the industry are scanning job listings and searching for creative ways to stay afloat while they wait for work. As unemployed carpenter Pat O'Connor told TIME Magazine: "It is a bad dream turning into a nightmare". He went on to ask grimly, "Is construction dead?"

The Construction Industry and the Internet

The increasingly central role of the Internet in modern society further imperils the struggling construction industry. The country is shopping, working and communicating online, eliminating the need for many storefront businesses and gradually closing them down. The popularity of online booksellers like Amazon.com finally brought Borders to its knees in February of 2011 after five years of cutbacks. The bankrupt company has let over 15,000 employees go and, after closing 200 stores, it expects to eliminate 6,000 more jobs in the coming months.

Once a home entertainment empire, Blockbuster Inc. filed for bankruptcy in September of 2010 after shutting down operations in Spain, Portugal and Peru and announcing it would sell all its European locations. Blockbuster lost its footing in the video rental market when online rentals—led by Netflix—started rivaling in-store pick-ups. Blockbuster's own online service never got off the ground like Netflix, which leapfrogged its biggest competitor when it launched instant streaming. In the United States, Blockbuster will shut down at least 1,000 locations in the next year, eliminating thousands of jobs, continuing the unemployment, foreclosure cycle. And not only does more unemployment mean higher foreclosure rates, it also adds to the nation's growing stockpile of empty commercial spaces. As buildings go vacant, a community's property value plummets, further discouraging new construction.

Economists project that in many areas of the country, employment will not return to pre-recession levels until 2030 or later. In the meantime, a new generation of American workers will be wrestling with job security in ways their parents never did. Whereas Baby Boomers were known to land jobs, plant roots and climb the company ladder over a period of 20-30 years, Generations X and Y represent a newly mobile workforce. Gold watches and company-funded pensions are things of the past. Mobile Internet technology like Wi-Fi, 3G access, laptops and smart phones makes it possible to work from home or on the road.

Access to the Internet through mobile technology also reduces the risk of entrepreneurship: starting a small business is more affordable than ever. Forget hiring a team and renting an office space. Companies big and small are eliminating their offices and outsourcing on a project-by-project basis to a pool of global professionals via online job marketplaces that allow individuals to bid on jobs.

Mobile lifestyles are flexible but they are certainly not mortgage-friendly. And people don't just want flexibility; they need it because, in a mobile culture, the possibility of relocation always lurks around the corner. Unsure where they will be in 5, 10, or 20 years, more families are opting to rent than buy. Afraid of being stuck with property they can't sell, potential homeowners are starting to feel that renting is a safer bet, at least while it remains a buyer's market.

What does this mean for the construction industry? Builders aren't building and home owners aren't remodeling—or even repairing. Statistically, renters are far less likely to fix or upgrade a home, even if it needs it and landlords will typically only address the most pressing problems. Meanwhile, the surge of start-up home businesses leaves commercial space up for grabs and commercial architects looking for work. Private sector construction work once accounted for 76% of the industry's revenue. That number has fallen by 16% and is still dropping, despite the fact that other industries are on the rebound.

The Future of Construction

According to the Associated General Contractors of America (AGC), construction spending has dropped 34% since the recession with few prospects for a quick revival. Along with detailed revenue employment statistics, the AGC also published recommendations for rebuilding the construction industry. If the industry is going to survive, it will have to evolve, which means making up for decreased demand by relying less on breaking new ground and focusing on different types of jobs altogether.

Energy retrofitting, improving a building's energy efficiency, is one way industry leaders see construction developing in the pre-recession economy and reviving private investment. The AGC is calling for Congress to establish tax credits that encourage energy efficient upgrades and the purchase of clean construction equipment. The AGC also hopes that removing trade barriers and restoring "Fast Track" trade promotion authority will stimulate demand for manufacturing and shipping facilities. The focus is on creatively ratcheting up private sector demand with tax relief and less red tape for both commercial investors and individual homeowners

Trade leaders point out that a recovery plan must take infrastructure delays, which are costing American businesses roughly $100 billion a year, into account. Federal highway construction, for example, has the potential to create upwards of 27,000 jobs for each $1 billion spent. But infrastructure stimulus plans have failed in the past, so legislators will have to think out of the box in order to avoid pumping tax dollars into projects without actually saving or creating jobs. The AGC enthusiastically supports President Obama's proposed fiscal 2012 budget, which calls for a $54 billion high-speed rail system and $336 billion in highway spending. If passed, the AGC says the budget could create as many as 10 million jobs in construction and related industries.

The economic world is much like the natural world in that in order to survive, you must evolve. For the construction industry to survive, it must adapt to the changing economic environment. Private demand is unlikely to return to pre-recession levels, which means the construction boom is over and many jobs will not be re-created. As foreclosures drain communities and Internet commerce squeezes stores out of business, millions of empty properties sit on the market, signaling an end to groundbreaking and permanent unemployment for scores of trades people. The construction industry's survival hinges on transforming to meet the needs of a changing society.

Today, most construction projects are focused on heavy infrastructure and public work: roads, bridges, schools, etc. In the coming years, as the green economy expands, "green collar jobs," work focused on reducing waste and pollution, are predicted to replace many lost construction jobs. Green collar workers build wind turbines instead of manufacturing plants and install solar panels instead of track lighting. Repairs and remodels will also slowly increase as the economy recovers, bolstering employment for some workers. Some trade leaders predict that construction is evolving from an industry bursting at the seams with jobs and employees to a niche field of experts and specialists.

Finally, for construction firms to survive, they must become more web-savvy. The Internet has changed the fabric of the global economy, of which construction is a lynchpin. Contractors and other trade leaders must be willing to embrace mobile technology in order to not be destroyed by it.

Construction has returned to its roots. Born out of necessity, building is once again a function of utility, not excess. Before the housing bubble burst, people were buying and trading homes with wild abandon, treating the world like a Monopoly board. In the post-recession world, property is no longer an investment, it's a liability. We can no longer afford to wait with bated breath for the construction industry to recover. In a post-recession, digital world, the construction worker waiting for a recovery will be waiting for a very long time.

6
The Painful Death of the Printing Industry

According to the Bureau of Labor Statistics, nearly 87,000 workers in the print publishing industry lost their jobs between the years 2009-2010; 4,200 in the month of November 2010 alone. This can partially be attributed to the recession, but it is not just a recent phenomenon. The print publishing industry, including books, magazines, newspapers, direct mail advertising and other printed media, has been suffering as a result of the growth of the internet for years. The decline in jobs in the industry is now becoming precipitous. In November 2010, major printing industry players such as Associated Press, Time Inc, Business Week and others reduced their staffs significantly, causing a drop in total employment in the sector to 776,800 compared to 863,600 in November 2009.

Obviously, the print publishing industry in the United States is in trouble, but it is also a global phenomenon. In the month of November 2009, Catalyst Paper, a major Canadian pulp and paper mill laid off over a thousand workers because of declining demand for paper. Catalyst Paper's vice president Brian Johnson stated that the major reason for the closure of the mill was the "structural decline in the market, where people are reading less, fewer papers" and the evolution of the internet as the major source of infotainment (Declining readership blamed for Job loss, Digital Journal).

Today, people prefer to communicate via email and get their news from online newspapers and blogs and are deviating away from traditional print sources. As a result, print media readership is declining significantly.

Many well established printing houses such as *Seattle Post-Intelligencer*, which was active for 146 years, have closed their doors because of declining advertising revenues. In the absence of funds, it became impossible to continue printing. The *Rocky Mountain News* in Colorado closed their offices and then the *San Francisco Chronicle* announced that it was reducing its printing operations in favor of expanding its online news delivery operations. In June of 2010, the century old Hawaii based newspaper, the *Honolulu Advertiser* printed its last Sunday Edition and closed down its presses after over a century of publication. As a result, over 400 journalists and other workers lost their jobs. (Last issue of Century Old Honolulu Newspaper, Digital Journal)

On the other side of the world, on Oct. 19, 2010, APN News & Media, publishers of the *New Zealand Herald* closed down its Manaku printing plant, causing 150 workers to lose their jobs. (APN to close Printing plant, NZ Herald)

This gloomy picture, while having gotten worse in recent years with the growth of the internet and, even more recently, the global recession, actually has earlier roots. The first threat posed to the printing industry came in the 1940s, with the birth of the television era. In 1945, when NBC began its ambitious news broadcasting program, newspapers began to face stiff competition and television entertainment began to replace reading as a leisure activity. Children began watching cartoons instead of reading comic books and grew up with television rather than with books. This trend continued into adulthood and today's parents and children overwhelmingly prefer TV and other forms of electronic entertainment over books. According to a 2006 report by CEEP (Center for Evaluation and Education Policy), book purchases by students is in continuous and rapid decline, having fallen 26.3% between the years 2004 to 2006. The report also mentioned that while the prices of printed books are continuously increasing, the number of staff members in libraries is decreasing regularly. (2006 trends of Library Services, CEEP)

While the printing industry as a whole was finding it difficult to compete with the attraction of television as the major public entertainment medium, the newspaper industry survived because people found it more satisfying to read local and regional news in more detailed format than national or international TV news channels offered. Viewers found that 30 second coverage of local and national news stories was not enough to satisfy their needs, so they continued to buy newspapers throughout the fifties, sixties, seventies and well into the nineties.

The first internet networks were established because of the ongoing technological competition between the US and USSR during the Cold War years. At the end of the Cold War, the new internet technology of internet opened up to more commercial ventures and started to establish itself as a dominant medium for advertising, news, entertainment, social networking and other modes of communication. People discovered that they could instantly send messages to their friends, relatives and colleagues, no matter how great the distances between them. As a result, they stopped writing letters; they had a better way to interact with each other. Not only they were able to send important information through emails, they could actually interact with each other through instant messaging. As a result, many workers in postal services became redundant. Whereas in the past, businesses relied on these services to deliver urgent printed documents, with the advent of internet, officials found a more secure and faster way of sharing data via the internet.

Between the decline in the book publishing industry, the newspaper industry, the magazine publishing industry and even the need for postal delivery services, the printing industry as a whole is involved in a losing battle, with its very survival at stake. Is there hope for the industry or is it doomed? A look at the history of the printing industry gives an understanding of why and how it grew and a look at the rise of new media gives an understanding of why the printing industry as a whole, once one of the world's most influential industries, will likely become a small, novelty niche in communications in the future.

The History of the Printing Press: A Glorious Past

Historians unanimously agree that the invention of the printing press by Johannes Gutenberg was one of the most significant events in human history. While the Chinese had invented a type of printing press several centuries before Gutenberg, it was his press, completed in 1440, that changed the face of the world. Gutenberg was not only an inventor but an entrepreneur and his Gutenberg Bible was the Western world's first "best seller." His invention led to the greatest mass dissemination of thought in history. Every discipline of human thought and endeavor, including religious, philosophical, political, economic and artistic, has been expanded and enriched by the printing press. It is what took Europe out of the Dark Ages and into the Enlightenment. It has resulted in wars and revolutions. It is largely responsible for the Protestant Reformation. The printing press can claim responsibility for advances in science and medicine. It has even been one of our major forms of entertainment.

In 1605, the world's first newspaper was printed by Johann Carolus. With the long-winded title of *Collection of All Distinguished and Commemorable News*, this German language paper paved the way for the great newspaper publishing companies that came later.

In the year 1641, Samuel Hartlib, a British social and cultural reformer, stated that "the art of printing will so spread knowledge that the common people, knowing their own rights and liberties, will not be governed by way of oppression." Governments and religious authorities tried to suppress the revolutionary effects of the printing press, but with only varying degrees of success. The printing press made it possible for the common man to study religious texts and politically important content freely without the controlling mediation of political and religious authorities. Before the invention of printing press, there was little incentive for the average person to even learn to read. The populace was largely dependent on clergymen and other authority figures, making control over them relatively easy. For this reason, most religious authorities throughout the world opposed the printing press. Despite their opposition, though, the presses continued to roll.

The printing press allowed idiosyncratic, revolutionary and radical thinkers to directly express their views and ideas in the public domain. It provided the required ammunition for radicals to bring about major social changes and revolutions, including the French and American Revolutions. It played a major role in removing the hierarchical system of absolute monarchy and kingships and supported the new system of Democratic government with the promise of transparency and freedom for the individual citizen to decide their own fate. The printing press played a major role in most of the revolutions, both peaceful and violent, throughout the world as it was the fastest manner to spread the ideas and viewpoints of the revolutionaries to the masses.

In 1895, the British historian, Lord Acton enthused that the printed word gave "assurance that the work of the Renaissance would last, that what was written would be accessible to all, that such an occultation of knowledge and ideas as had depressed the Middle Ages would never recur, that not an idea would be lost." He was right, but he failed to foresee the coming of the digital age.

The Diminishing Impact of the Printing Press

Today, information technology in general and the internet in particular has emerged as the next great revolution in communications. Word processors connected to printers have made it possible to write, proofread, edit and print documents from a home or office based computer far more quickly and easily than these documents could be produced in the past. The internet has made it possible to share those documents with the world at the click of a button. If you want information, your mobile device, laptop or PC contains more information than the largest library in the world and most of it is freely available. While nobody disputes that the internet is the greatest revolution in communications since the invention of the printing press, this time, it comes at a human cost. Before Gutenberg's press, there were no rival communications industries except perhaps for highly skilled scribes, whose penmanship and literacy was in demand for transcribing legal documents and religious texts. This was a relative handful of skilled craftsmen, though.

The internet, on the other hand, came after over five centuries of dominance of the printing industry. As it replaces the printed word as our dominant means of written communication, it is costing tens of thousands of jobs. Whereas the printing press created hundreds of thousands of jobs over the centuries, computer technology and the internet is going to cost far more jobs than it creates because so much of the process of creating even printed materials has been automated.

Across the board, groups and individuals who want to disseminate information now do so via the internet. When it is so inexpensive, easy and effective to publish ebooks, videos and other informative content online, there is simply no need to use the printed page anymore. Everyone from radical anarchists to evangelical Christians now use the internet as their primary means of communication. It doesn't matter how large or how small the organization is, the internet is a faster, cheaper and more versatile means of communication than any seen before in history. Along with the lack of need for print media has come a precipitous loss of jobs throughout the entire printing industry. There is less need for pulp mills, printing presses, editors, publishers and other printing industry personnel now that the world is turning to the internet to both create information and disseminate it.

Jobs in the printing industry cost employers money and those costs are passed on to consumers. The internet, in comparison, is very cheap and many concerns can offer newspapers, online magazines ("zines") and other content for free that subscribers formerly had to pay for. When they do charge a subscription fee, it is minimal compared to the cost of a newspaper or magazine subscription. Content providers make their money indirectly through advertising revenues generated by Google Adwords, affiliate links and other advertising sources. When the consumer can get the information he wants and needs for free, he is not likely to turn back to newspapers, magazines and books.

The Diminishing Impact of the Printed Word in Society

Along with the dissemination of printed material came widespread literacy. The general populace had a hunger to learn and with that hunger came the desire to learn to read and write and pass these skills on to their children. This in turn led to an even greater expansion of the printing industry as books, pamphlets and illustrated children's books were produced to feed popular culture's hunger.

Another outgrowth of widespread literacy was the increasing need for postal services for the average person. Between the need for news services to increase their circulation, businesses and governments to transfer documents over long distances and individuals to send letters and documents to friends, relatives and colleagues in distant places, an organized way to deliver those tens of thousands of documents was required. In the United States, Benjamin Franklin was appointed as the first Postmaster General in 1775. Early postal delivery systems began with the famed Pony Express. After the transcontinental railway service was put into operation, letters could be delivered from New York to San Francisco in a matter of days.

The invention of the typewriter in the mid nineteenth century did little damage to the printing industry as a whole because with a typewriter, only one page at a time could be written. If multiple copies were needed, only a printing press could efficiently do the job. In fact, the typewriter was arguably a boon to the printing industry, since it led to increased output from writers and hence increased publication of books. The typewriter definitely made the United States Postal Service busier, as businesses hired typists to transcribe all of their important documents, which were then mailed to clients and colleagues throughout the country and overseas.

The well established postal service created even more jobs for the printing industry as businesses started using these services for bulk advertising purposes. For decades, this was one of the cheapest forms of advertising for companies. The only competition, in fact, was expensive radio and television advertising which only the largest corporations could afford and newspaper advertising, which was used as a supplement to bulk mailings. Obviously this was good news for everyone in the printing industry.

For decades, the postal service was the predominant means of transport of the printed word. Then came the internet. In the past decade alone, penmanship has become a virtually lost art as a new generation has become expert at using email and social media for communication. Postcards are quaint relics that people occasionally send to loved ones just for their novelty value. Full-fledged letters are almost a thing of the past. Why waste your precious vacation time laboriously writing a letter and waiting for your photographs to be developed when you can simply type an email or post a message on Facebook, complete with a digital photo album? When Christmas rolls around, you can send your loved ones a clever online Christmas card rather than go to the trouble of buying cards and going to the post office to mail them.

Whereas "junk mail" and catalogs used to be the dominant form of cheap advertising, the internet is even cheaper and it reaches a larger audience. Since people get their magazines online, there is no longer a significant need for the postal service to deliver magazine subscriptions. "Spam" is the junk mail of today, but unlike its older counterpart, which was either used to light the fire or put straight into the recycling bin, spam is sorted out and deleted from your email "trash can." There is no paper involved and no waste of resources.

You name it and if it has to do with the printed word, it is losing its appeal. Very few people look in the classifieds sections of what regional newspapers remain for jobs. They don't announce their weddings in the paper, nor do they publish death announcements. They don't look for the latest information on the stock market in the paper and they don't look for cars or real estate in the paper either. If you want to see a movie, you check out what's playing online and reserve your seat while you're there. The same thing applies to travel plans. Why look in the paper or go to a travel agency for a brochure when you can get all of the information you need online? In our day-to-day personal lives, the printing press and the postal service are already all but redundant.

In 1994, Robert J. McGovern developed a job seeking software company he called NetStart Inc. His venture was successful enough that within a few years a consortium of newspapers got together and created their own online job search facilities. While it may seem like a counterproductive move for newspaper giants like the New York Times and the Los Angeles Times, they were really just seeing the writing on the wall and keeping up with the times. Successful newspaper publishers are pragmatists first and foremost. They are not going to stick with printing newspapers out of a sense of nostalgia or pride if in doing so it is going to put them out of business. The fact that these major newspapers began their online services in the nineties certainly accelerated the demise of the printing industry, but it probably saved their businesses. Today, smaller newspapers that clung to their proud heritages of over a century are simply closing their doors and disappearing because they didn't get in on the internet revolution quickly or aggressively enough.

Vulnerability of the Printing Press

The printing industry is not yet dead. It remains a major business sector globally. According to some estimates, more than 45 trillion pages were printed in the year 2005. Around 30,700 printing companies were working in the United States in the year 2006. In the *2006 U.S. Industry & Market Outlook*, Barnes Reports suggested that the printing industry had assets of $112 billion.

Despite its enormity, the printing industry is in rapid decline. In the year 2009, 105 newspapers were shut down while more than 10,000 jobs were lost in the newspaper industry. The market data further reveals that in the year 2009, newspapers and printed magazines lost a 30% share of print ad sales. In addition, the top 23 newspapers of the United States reported that their newspaper circulation declined by 7% to 20%. In the year 2010, 61 newspapers closed in the first half of the year alone (*The Year the Newspaper Died*, Preethi Dumpala). While it is true that one of the reasons for this precipitous decline was the recession, this trend suggests that even if the market recovers, the printing industry is unlikely to gain its lost glory.

The internet is relentlessly eating up the major share of print ad sales. Even at the height of the recession, internet giants like Google made huge profits and the major source of Google's profits come from their ad revenues. More and more people are taking part in internet business activities because of its greater reach, better facilities and cheap rates. Instead of investing in printed advertising, they invest in internet advertising, SEO and other web based advertising strategies.

Another influence that is causing a decline in demand for printed materials is the increasing "green revolution." Wasted paper is seen as having a negative effect on the environment, while the internet's environmental effect is perceived to be negligible. Whether this is entirely true or not is beside the point: it is perceived to be true, therefore a significant number of environmentally conscious consumers are turning away from books and magazines to ereaders and other electronic devices. Because a single ereader such as the Amazon Kindle can carry an entire library of books in one device, collectively, ebook readers can theoretically save hundreds of forests. This, combined with the fact that ebooks are cheaper than their printed counterparts is leading to an explosion in the popularity of Kindles and other ereaders.

The Internet and Education

In the past, every family had at least one dictionary in the home and having a set of Encyclopedias was considered something of a status symbol. Both of these are now noticeable by their absence in the home today. In their place, people simply use an online dictionary and Wikipedia has largely replaced the traditional encyclopedia. MSN Encarta, Encyclopedia Britannica and other encyclopedias are available as CDs or via the internet, though even these are losing their market share. Not only are online encyclopedias free to use, they contain far more information than can possibly be printed in a set of encyclopedias. Furthermore, the information is always up-to-date.

The one place where printed material would seem to be indispensable would be in schools and universities. While it's true that some textbooks are still required, they are rapidly being supplanted by digital media. In fact, with the soaring cost of a university education, tens of thousands of students are turning to full time online universities for their degrees. In many instances, virtually all study materials are available online, tests and exams are taken online and the only time the student has to make a physical appearance at his chosen university is to attend labs. While as yet, the demand for textbooks has not entirely disappeared, the internet has already taken its toll on the demand for textbooks and other printed study materials.

Recently, the Massachusetts Institute of Technology offered

a unique way for national and international students to pursue their education with the help of internet by offering all its courses online. MIT has been providing online courses, including all related study and research material, for its students and it is becoming an increasingly popular trend and is seen as a better, cheaper and easier method to pursue your studies. (*For Exposure, Universities Put Courses on the Web*, The New York Times).

After making a deal with OpenCourseWave Consortium in 2001, MIT announced that it was putting its entire course catalog online. The global Open Educational Resources Movement is making it possible for anyone who wishes to get an education to do so online. There is no need for textbooks because everything is available online freely or very inexpensively. Obviously, this increasing trend, welcome as it may be, is taking a major toll on the printing industry.

Children's books and comic books are suffering the same fate as text books. Whereas reading to the children used to be a vital part of being a parent, today it is a dying tradition. Trading comic books was a growing up ritual in earlier generations, but today the superheroes of comic books are all in computer games, DVDs and films. Spiderman, Superman and other comic book characters are still very popular, but they are watched on television, YouTube or another online video service provider.

Print on Demand Publishing

Print on demand (also known as publishing on demand) is the publishing industry's version of "lean manufacturing," a process whereby goods are manufactured faster, but in smaller quantities than was formerly the case. Thanks to improved logistics and digitized printing processes, a book that is ordered online or from a brick and mortar shop can be printed "on demand" and shipped to its destination in a matter of days - sometimes even less.

There are many advantages to this system. For one thing, it reduces waste, since the printer doesn't have to print books in large quantities in order to keep the cost per book down. For another, it saves the publisher a great deal of money because he doesn't have to mark down unsold books and take a loss on overstock. The advent of digital printing has made print on demand possible. There is virtually no setup time at all involved. An order arrives for 5 (or 50) copies of one title and a few of another. The printer then passes the orders directly to the printing "press" (which is no press at all). Without hesitation, the "press" will produce the required numbers of books for each title. There is no setup time, much less typesetting, involved at all. The cover, the contents and even the binding of each title is all programmed into the printing process.

The internet has made print on demand publications more popular than ever because it gives self-publishers a way to print and distribute their own titles. Online publishers like Lulu provide customers with all the tools they need to produce their books and even distribute them online. Print on demand is becoming a real threat to book publishers because even many established writers are now marketing their own self published books online rather than going through traditional publishers.

All of this should be good news for the printing industry. If thousands of writers are now self publishing hard copies of books, then the printing presses should be kept humming. To a degree this is true, but the catch is that while they are printing books, these new "printing presses" require almost no staff to operate and only a few staff members to sort, pack and box up the books for mailing.

Another problem with the new breed of author who uses the print on demand option is that they also offer their books in digital format. Amazon, the largest seller of books in the world, now offers software for self-publishers that allows them to format their books for the Kindle reading device. Then they can offer them for sale on Amazon and promote them through their own website, Craig's list, Ebay and social media outlets. There is no reason to produce printed materials to promote their books at all, unless they also distribute them in bookshops. In that case, they can produce promotional literature on their home PC and print it up on their home printer. Between this and the fact that if an author wishes to have a single copy of his book printed instead of having to pay for a thousand, the actual number of books being printed "on demand" is very limited and the need for commercial printing companies is, by extension, also very limited.

The Final (Digital) Word

Short of pulling the plug on the internet and outlawing the use of computer technology, there is virtually no hope for the printing industry and related jobs in the future. Of course, there will always be limited demand for books, magazines, brochures and other printed materials, but the key word there is "limited." There is still a "limited" demand for 33 rpm records, too, but whereas in the past these were produced in the millions, they are now pressed in small batches by boutique recording studios. Similarly, in the very near future books are going to be published on demand only for those old-fashioned readers who remember the pleasure of sitting down with a good book. It is not likely that the children of Generation X or Y are going to feel any nostalgia for printed books any more than they long for the return of the 33 rpm recording.

Few would argue that turning away from costly and environmentally damaging books made from paper is a bad omen for the future, but the question remains: where are the tens of thousands of workers involved in the printing industry going to find jobs? When a pulp mill shuts down, the workers can't walk into an Amazon warehouse and ask for a job because those warehouses are so automated they need very few workers anyway. An executive at a publishing house or newspaper won't find a job at an online publishing house unless he happens to be a computer whiz. His existing skills are no longer needed. Those workers who lose their jobs at the large printing companies won't find jobs elsewhere because they are not being created. Automation eats up any jobs that may otherwise have been created in a modern printing facility that manages to survive.

Can all of these workers find something to do in the retail outlets that sell books and magazines? Since all the major book and magazine sellers like Borders and Barnes and Noble are closing many outlets and downsizing others, it's not likely. Book and magazine sales are way down and the big booksellers are investing in their online activities rather than their brick and mortar outlets. Arguably, if it weren't for their increased online sales, some of these companies would already be bankrupt.

What is happening to the communications industries today is at least as momentous as what happened back in the 15th century when Johannes Gutenberg introduced the printing press to the world. It can be argued that there was no downside to Gutenberg's invention. Not only did the printing press lead to the enlightenment and education of tens of millions of people over the course of the centuries, it also created tens of millions of jobs. While digital communications are spreading literacy and ideas throughout the world, there is a downside to them: they are costing jobs. In the distant future, this may lead to improved living conditions for the average person, but it won't come until after a long and painful period of adjustment. It will be interesting to see what historians have to say about the digital age in fifty or a hundred years' time. One thing is almost certain, though - our descendants won't be reading what the historians have to say in books.

7
The New Age of Advertising

Over the past three centuries, the North American advertising industry has evolved from a static mechanism that educates and entertains the vast buying public to a living organism that must interact with and respond to each individual client. The lights are flickering on Madison Avenue as technology renders print media obsolete and the great ad behemoths of a dying age struggle to digitize. The rise of the Internet has changed the face of Main Street forever and the role of the advertiser has adapted from starting conversations to participating in them, making today's marketing moguls difficult to separate from their customers. Fifty years ago the advertising industry underwent a creative revolution; today it is facing an apocalypse as social media, viral marketing, and crowd sourcing blur the lines between advertiser and consumer, eradicating hundreds of thousands of jobs in the process.

The History of the Advertising Industry in North America

The roots of traditional North American advertising can be traced back to British mercantilism. Colonization flooded England with exotic goods from all over the world, most of which were unfamiliar to the vast buying public. In order to recover their investments, merchants hung illustrative signs and distributed trade cards and handbills to educate potential clients about their products. Early North American colonial merchants continued the practice of using trade cards to promote their wares, hiring artists to design whimsical print images advertising everything from spices to horse blankets. Leaflets espousing the virtuous, even miraculous properties of a particular product wooed literate, upper-class consumers and traveling salesmen captured the rural market, tailoring their pitches to each potential customer they visited.

However, word-of-mouth advertising was expensive and inefficient and as merchants began to sense the limited potential of direct marketing methods, they turned to print media, which was just beginning to take off at the turn of the 18th century. *The Boston News-Letter*, considered the original North American newspaper, published its first advertisement in 1704; a few bare lines of text about a luxury estate on long Island. In 1729, Benjamin Franklin took newspaper advertising a step further by adding illustrations to the pages of "new advertisements" he included in the *Pennsylvania Gazette:* his first publishing venture. He went on to found America's first daily paper, the *Pennsylvania Packet & Daily Advertiser*, whose vast readership changed advertising forever by allowing sellers to reach previously unreachable masses.

Though some pioneer 19th century publishers were skeptical of print marketing, limiting ad space or banning sales notices completely, the newly industrialized printing press churned out more than 5,000 newspapers and magazines, making print media the main way that merchants, entrepreneurs, and manufacturers generated sales. Thus, the American advertising agency was born in 1843 to Volney B. Palmer in Philadelphia. At the end of the 19th century, N.W. Ayer & Son bought Palmer out and began hiring artistic talent, single-handedly creating America's newest profession, the advertising executive and foreshadowing the traditional advertising agency's transition from brokerage firm to full-service business.

Following Ayer's lead, by 1861 over 20 agencies had sprouted up in New York City alone, with dozens more taking root in Philadelphia, Boston, and Chicago. Patent medicine manufacturers dominated most client rosters but that quickly changed as the public began to tire of the "quackery" or false claims for which such products were made famous. Meanwhile, the advent of branding placed packaged goods in the advertising spotlight. Newly branded products like Ivory soap, Uneeda biscuits, and Colgate toothpaste replaced their generic bulk counterparts, doing away with the custom of bringing one's own containers to the general store. And with branding came slogans; N.W. Ayer led the way in 1898 with the million-dollar catch phrase, "Do You Know Uneeda Biscuit?"

Aaron Montgomery Ward pioneered the mail-order catalog in 1872, capitalizing on a niche of rural consumers who were skeptical of "middlemen" and more interested in ordering their goods straight from Chicago. Sears, Roebuck and Co., was quick to follow suit, piggybacking on Montgomery Ward's success and establishing itself as "the Consumers' Bible" within a few short decades.

With the dawn of the 20th century came the regulation of advertising standards, abating some of the consumer skepticism that helped Ward's and Sears reap billions and confirming that the advertising professional was here to stay, at least for the next 100 years. After the 1906 passage of the Pure Food and Drug Act sparked a slew of lawsuits against companies like Coca-Cola for purportedly mislabeling products, the National Better Business Bureau formed with the mission of establishing a culture of truth in advertising. Two years later, Congress established the Federal Trade Commission to further protect consumers against harmful business practices. Soon thereafter, agencies, advertisers, and media representatives came together to create the American Association of Advertising Agencies, which helped further legitimize the industry. At the same time, visionaries like Walter Dill Scott added layers to the increasingly complex relationship between advertiser and consumer with the publication of his book, *The Psychology of Advertising in Theory and Practice,* which many credit as the fount of modern market research as well as the original guide to helping marketers tap into their target audience's desires.

The 1920s saw the first big advertising revolution in nearly two centuries with the advent of public radio broadcasting. In 1920, the nation's first radio station, KDKA of Pittsburgh, announced Warren G. Harding's presidency for a small Pennsylvania listening population. Six years later, the National Broadcasting Co. debuted and not too long after, WNBC broadcast the first radio advertisement: a step that "liberated advertising from its relationship to literacy." Marketers soon began experimenting with jingles and radio plays and it wasn't long before America's favorite programs bore brands in their titles, like "Kraft Music Hall" and the "Hallmark Hall of Fame." By 1938, radio was the top marketing medium in the country and thousands of people were employed to develop advertising for the airwaves.

By the early 1950s, commercial television had made its debut.

In the blink of the eye, television surpassed radio, newspaper, and magazines as the largest advertising medium in the world as well as a prosperous fount of employment. Once video recording came on the scene, the 30-second spot established itself as the backbone of the advertising industry. Over fifty years later, television advertising is yet to be knocked from its throne, though many would argue that it is quickly growing ripe for succession.

Inspired by the industry's rapid expansion into multi-sensory territory, the agency of Doyle, Dayne, and Bernbach made advertising history when it originated the concept of the creative team in 1959, pairing art directors and copywriters for the first time ever. The resulting "Think Small" campaign for Volkswagen is still considered the industry's greatest success. In the years to follow, DDB and similarly inspired agencies continued to expand the standard creative team to include musicians, social scientists, and psychologists: establishing advertising as a sound career path for budding professionals. The years surrounding DDB's monumental invention are known as the advertising industry's "Creative Revolution," spawning such legendary campaigns as the Marlboro Man, "Good to the last drop" for Maxwell House, and "We Try Harder" for Avis. AMC's celebrated television series, *Mad Men*, is set during this era of American advertising, chronicling the career of fictional ad man, Don Draper, who frequently references Bill Bernbach, one of DDB's three famous founders.

Until recently, the creative team that DDB dreamed up back in advertising's heyday remained the keystone of modern marketing. Their demise began with the shift away from mass marketing, which had ruled since the beginning of the 20th century, caused by the arrival of cable television in the 1970s. According to William M. O'Barr, author of *Culture and the Ad: Exploring Otherness in the World of Advertising*, "broadcasting became narrowcasting" nearly overnight.

In the 1990s, the marketer's ability to zero in on a desired demographic led to decentralization, chipping away at the mammoth agencies that had grown to epic proportions during the "buying binge" of the 1980s. Boutique firms offering specialized niche services threatened agency loyalty and dozens of big names like Ameritech Corp. and General Mills began opening accounts with regional advertisers and media companies. Scrambling to regain lost ground, when the Internet left the academic realm and became a public commodity in the mid-1990s, agencies turned to integrated marketing techniques, offering promotion, public relations, and online advertising in addition to traditional services.

The surge in Internet commerce, reaching $8 billion by the end of the 20th century, led experts to question whether the World Wide Web would swallow up TV, radio, and newspaper dollars forever. When the dot-com bubble burst in 2000, the industry breathed a collective sigh of relief. A little over a decade later, as thousands of unemployed advertising professionals troll the Classifieds, it is becoming obvious that this relief may have been a bit premature.

Advertising In the Age of Individualism

Before eCommerce took a new millennial nose dive, it seemed like the whole world wanted a piece of the World Wide Web: the 20th century's equivalent of the gold rush. In her 2000 essay, *The Wild, Wild Web: The Mythic American West and the Electronic Frontier*. Helen McClure writes, "If a frontier implies commercial exploitation, then 1999 was for the Web what 1849 was for California. Suddenly everyone headed for cyberspace, scrambling to stake their claim to a domain name before someone else grab[bed] it, hoping to strike it rich on the e-frontier."

Just as Western expansion changed life in North America forever, "the Cyberspace Rush" dramatically altered how people lived, worked, and socialized, not only in North America but all over the globe. And as the World Wide Web expanded, the world itself seemed to shrink. Email collapsed distances, allowing anyone with Internet access to instantly communicate with other users, no matter how far away. Message boards and chat rooms suddenly made global networking possible. And eCommerce "diminishe[d] the economic consequences of geographic distance to insignificant levels," establishing a "level playing field" for small and medium-size businesses. By reducing the speed and cost of communication, the Internet accelerated daily life for the majority of industrialized society.

Little was left unchanged by the smaller, faster world created by the World Wide Web; least of all the advertising industry. Shiny new platforms for consuming, working, and socializing necessitated new ways of reaching out to the buying public. But it was a pair of software developers, not advertising professionals, who led the way, foreshadowing the 21st century swap of the marketing mogul for the tech wizard. In 1996, while working on the initial plans for JavaSoft, Sabeer Bhatia and Jack Smith accidentally stumbled upon the Internet innovation that would completely transform modern communication: free Web-based email. Within months, their discovery went public when Hotmail was born.

Despite a meager advertising budget, Hotmail picked up 20,000 subscribers in its first month. Less than six months later, the number grew to over a million. By early 1998, Bhatia and Smith's happy accident boasted more than 12 million subscribers and it achieved those numbers without blasting TV, radio, and print with expensive promotions. Traditional marketers gaped at Hotmail's runaway success, wondering what type of spell its founders had cast to garner the type of consumer interest of which industry greats only dreamed.

The secret was simple. Below the signature line, each Hotmail message arrived in its recipient's inbox with an invitation to "Get your free-email at Hotmail." Thus, contemporary "viral marketing" was born, though the term wasn't coined for over a year after the "webolutionary" product arrived on the scene. In reality, viral marketing was nothing more than an online twist on a classic technique, better known as word-of-mouth marketing. Hotmail's founders didn't need to spend their capital on pricey promotions because their subscribers did the job for them, spreading the company's success like a virus each time they sent an email. Meanwhile, a couple of humble software developers were fast becoming Silicon Valley's first millionaires through banner ads and advanced service fees. Thanks to Hotmail, nearly two centuries after it went out of style, direct marketing was back with a vengeance.

Clickstream data, information recording the Web pages users

frequented and the time they spent there, offered companies priceless insights into their prospective clients' online preferences. Just as cable television led to more efficient marketing, allowing firms to zero in on their target demographic via specialty channels, user profiling techniques based on computer-generated data sets narrowed the focus even further. The speed and precision with which clickstream data was collected slashed the price of market research, largely doing away with lengthy surveys and expensive teams of analysts. Thus, while companies like Hotmail were thriving, fewer advertising professionals were actually working. Because clickstream data is digitally processed and analyzed, only a handful of individuals need to oversee the process. It didn't take long for companies to realize that reduced personnel meant targeted banner ads based on clickstream data were both more effective and more affordable than classic forms of direct marketing, driving down traditional advertising spending as well as employment, click by click.

As viral marketing and banner advertising grew, companies quickly learned that it was no longer profitable to blast advertisements for their one size fits all products at the masses. Furthermore, eCommerce created a consumer expectation of "made for me" products and services that was only further reinforced by direct marketing. What would have been completely economically unviable a few short years earlier, catering to each consumer with custom-targeted goods and marketing messages, became a crucial criterion for a company's success.

At the same time that direct marketing techniques tailored for individual consumers were resurfacing in advertising culture, popular culture was also heading into an Age of Individualism, validating the maxim of famous historian, Daniel J. Boorstin: "Advertising is the rhetoric of democracy." Like Hotmail, Web hosts like GeoCities and Tripod made free home pages available starting in the mid-1990s, giving Internet users a platform to promote themselves and share personal details with the wider Web world. The online diary community, OpenDiary, hailed by many as the precursor to the modern blog, debuted in 1998, becoming an instant phenomenon. By the new millennium, GeoCities was a close third to AOL and

Yahoo in terms of visits and OpenDiary was fighting off competitors like LiveJournal and Xanga, whose combined users currently number into the billions.

The success of such communities sparked the Web 2.0 wildfire that spread rapidly throughout the first decade of the 21st century and is still spreading today. The crux of Web 2.0 is interactivity and information sharing instead of "static screenfulls." The open source encyclopedia Wikipedia led the way in 2001, inviting users to participate in cataloging world knowledge. Over the next few years, the groundwork laid by GeoCities and OpenDiary gave way to social networking sensations like Friendster, MySpace, and Facebook: interactive, user-based communities where individuals come together around shared interests, contacts, or experiences. Shortly thereafter, the content communities YouTube and Flickr came on the scene, providing a public space for people to display personal photos and videos.

Web 2.0 turned the Internet into a dynamic social arena, changing how society interacts and shares information. What does this mean for marketing? "It's all about participating, sharing, and collaboration, rather than straightforward advertising and selling," write Andreas M. Kaplan and Michael Haenlein in their 2010 article, *Users of the world, unite! The challenges and opportunities of Social Media*. Today's savviest marketers know that, if they want their message to be heard, advertising must be a dialog, not a monologue. Companies like Starbucks get the picture. The "My Starbucks Idea" campaign asks customers to brainstorm ways to improve their coffee-drinking experience and then calls for a vote. Other companies like Pepsi, Mentos, and Pepto-Bismol have gone viral, seeking creative YouTube videos starring their products and promising cash prizes and TV exposure as rewards. If just one user-generated video makes it big on a site like Facebook, the viral campaign will have succeeded, all with minimal financial investment on the part of the benefiting company and fewer employees on the part of the agency.

With its emphasis on autonomy and personal choice, the Age of Individualism has made the buying public resentful of being marketed to: today's consumer wants to feel in control of their purchasing decisions. Google has the concept down pat, having spawned a brand new type of marketing using the success of its search engine. Businesses utilize search engine marketing to attract potential clients to their site based on search results. Paid search engine marketing programs like Google AdWords offer companies the opportunity to pay for search terms that trigger advertising messages on the same screen displaying a user's search results. Similarly, Google AdSense places subtle advertising messages on customer websites, their content derived from geographical location and high-value keywords. Though its immense popularity has inspired companies like Yahoo and Microsoft to develop similar programs, Google remains the world leader in search engine marketing.

On the information superhighway, each user is in the driver's seat, free to choose his or her unique route to information, communication, and entertainment. Nowadays, to digitize is to survive but it takes even more to thrive. Companies can no longer afford to view the buying public as a homogeneous group of objects ready to be plied with jingles and catch phrases. The era of the Internet is about interactivity and immediacy. It's not enough to talk. If today's marketers want their message heard, they must be ready to listen.

The Death of Don Draper or Out With the Ad Executive and In With the Tech Guru

Before the Internet, access to entertainment, news, and business statistics was predictable and controlled. Advertisers marked their calendars with newspaper and magazine publication schedules and set their watches to radio, television, and cinema lineups. Much like a media buffet, the public could choose from an assortment of options without ever setting foot in the kitchen. In those days, the 30-second TV spot was the ad agency's main dish with a newspaper or magazine spread on the side. But since the world went online, everything has changed. The media buffet has lost its appeal. Consumers aren't content for companies to feed them messages. They want to be part of the process and the Internet hands them the tools.

For example, the availability of online video libraries like Hulu and SideReel mean that fewer families have to pencil their favorite television shows into their household agendas. The Internet makes it possible for the individual viewer to be their own programmer, choosing when and where they watch a newly-released movie or a show's latest episode. This is a shift that chips away at the cornerstone of the 30-second spot. Of course, some companies can get around this by paying to be among the lucky few whose ads air on Hulu-inspired sites. However, this scheme leaves small businesses out and shrinks the amount of advertisers that can reach a particular audience. And if users grate at mainstream media altogether, they can dodge commercials completely and head to YouTube or Veoh, where artists showcase their independent web series and films for free.

As people pay more attention to each other and less attention to agency-generated advertising pitches, the inevitable consequence is a major shift in the way marketers reach out to potential customers as well as what companies seek in an agency. When the 30-second spot was king, agencies guarded their talent like gold, searching far and wide for the perfect pieces to add to their creative collections and then charging clients exorbitant rates to access them. Internet culture, on the other hand, is based on sharing and interactivity, as well as urgency. Thus, crowd-sourcing, the practice of contracting a single employee's task to a large community, is a natural step in the evolution of the advertising industry. No longer bound to a particular agency, companies can take their pick from a vast ocean of freelance professionals, amateur bloggers or both, depending on where they are advertising and to whom.

Old Spice had wild success with this hybrid approach in its 2010 viral campaign which began with a few traditional spots featuring the amusing "Old Spice man" and then quickly made its way to the Facebook, Twitter, and YouTube. Fans were told that when they Tweeted about the Old Spice man, he may just return the favor with a personalized video. Old Spice carefully chose recipients of its customized "adutainment" in order to maximize views and Internet users loved it. In a few days' time, Old Spice had garnered nearly

700,000 Facebook fans, successfully updating its aging image while slashing its advertising budget in the process.

Now that crowd-sourcing has come on the scene, an agency that stakes an exclusive claim to the next big idea will quickly be laughed off by its newly-digitized clients. In a recent *Fast Company* article entitled, *The Future of Advertising*, Evan Fry of Victors & Spoils describes the advertising industry's reaction to the new world of mass collaboration: "I think the new model is scary because all of us in the ad industry want to feel, at least from a creative point of view, that we have something no one else has." The new model is also scary because it means the end of many longstanding client-agency relationships and, with it, massive layoffs of advertising professionals. The Don Draper type executive has become something akin to a living dinosaur: a beloved relic of the past but certainly not a beacon of the future.

When compared to digital agencies founded on crowd-sourcing principles, the traditional advertising agency is expensive and inefficient. And clients are catching on, which explains why so many big names like Kraft Foods and Nike are cutting ties with the agencies they once swore by. In *The Future of Advertising*, *Fast Company* describes one such digital agency, GeniusRocket, as "what an ad agency looks like when it's stripped of Madison Avenue skyscrapers, high-priced creatives on payroll, sushi dinners at Nobu, and two-week shoots at the Viceroy in Santa Monica." What's left is a "bare-bones website that crowd-sources broadcast-ready TV ads from a pool of loosely vetted talent from Poland to Guam." Apparently, the model works. Kraft Foods, once loyal to JWT for nearly 80 years, "fell in love" with one of GeniusRocket's crowd-sourced ads and hired them on the spot.

What does all this mean for advertising professionals? Widespread unemployment: a harsh reality made even harsher by the recent recession. When stocks plummeted, so did a great majority of advertising budgets, leading to the loss of more than 160,000 industry jobs in a two year period as well as the permanent closure of legendary firms like Lehman Brothers, Pearson, and the Chicago branch of JWT. Hoping to do more with less, many companies took advantage of the Web 2.0 explosion and concentrated their efforts on search marketing and social media, two methods that require less spending and even less personnel. This was good news for businesses, but very bad news for the advertising industry.

In the aftermath of the recession, the Nevada Commission on Tourism fought a reduced budget with an advertising overhaul that re-focused the state's efforts on social media and viral marketing. "By delivering simple messages and gaining accessibility to leading new media sites, the states has cut costs and gotten more return on investment," reports the *Las Vegas Sun*. According to an article published on December 8, 2010, for every dollar that Nevada spends, it sees $31 in media exposure, as opposed to the $17/dollar it received before making the shift. While the state used to pump all its advertising dollars into traditional strategies, it now only dabbles in TV and print ads, channeling most of its budget into a "fast and flexible" approach that includes real-time mobile updates on snow conditions and cheaply produced YouTube videos publicizing local happenings like Reno's La Tomatino food fight. Nevada's new approach has worked wonders for the state's economy but not necessarily for its advertising professionals, who experienced widespread layoffs consistent with their peers around the country.

The cutbacks aren't limited to just creative staff, either. Agency planners, analysts, and media buyers face unemployment as automation, software, and digital measuring make their jobs obsolete. Public relations consultants are also in jeopardy as companies turn to search engine marketing to fix their PR woes. Pre-Internet, if a business wanted to revive or rescue its reputation, it fought negative press with a strategic news conference or press release. In the post-WWW world, the press is the least of a business's concerns. Companies must now contend with blogs, social networks, and review communities where users, unlike media sources, don't have to worry about a big name client yanking their sponsorship. Thus, in many cases, the job goes to Google to clean up the mess instead of a team of PR professionals.

There is no better example of this than the disastrous Deepwater Horizon oil spill that gushed for three months, tarnishing BP's reputation as it destroyed the Gulf Coast. BP went from spending roughly $57,000 a month on Google search results to just under $3.6 million. And that was just in the month of June. In a September 2010 article on Google spending, Michael Learmonth of *Advertising Age* explained that "BP's increase underscores how important Google has become for reputation management in the battle for public opinion." Will Margiloff of Innovation Interaction was quoted as calling Google the "remote control for the world; it's the first stop, not TV."

Many say that Google's success negates the advertising industry's doomsday cries; a statement that is not entirely untrue, though it is misleading. Google generates new jobs every day and its AdWords headquarters, right outside of Detroit, is credited with rescuing the dying city from complete collapse. It's undeniable that Google has contributed to the advertising industry's recent revival. As of early 2010, *Advertising Age* declared that the worst was officially over and ZenithOptimedia predicts that the industry will grow by 4.6% this year and 5.2% in the two years that follow.

But that doesn't mean that unemployed advertising professionals should expect their jobs back anytime soon. Newspaper and magazine advertising is expected to fall 2% by 2013, meaning sudden death for thousands of print advertisers. And though TV remains in the lead, internet spending is riding its tail. Internet marketing will rise by 48% in the next three years, the effect of which will almost certainly be larger unemployment lines for traditional advertising professionals.

Who should we expect to find in their place? The answers lie in the Help Wanted ads, which are typically short on advertising listings and overflowing with calls for web designers, tech gurus, and software engineers. If companies want to keep up, they need mobile applications and social games, not just TV spots. This is unfamiliar territory for traditional advertising professionals, the majority of whom are ill-equipped even for software brainstorming sessions.

And internet leaders like Google and Facebook aren't willing to wait. Famous for snatching up successful startups instead of taking the time to develop talent from within, Google and its peers do little to hide their hurry. Google senior manager David Lawee explains: "If you bring smart people who also have domain expertise and ask them to solve the problem...you're just accelerating things that much faster. That's why I come to the conclusion that we'll do more...acquisitions." This does not offer much hope for traditional advertising professionals who are considering making a transition to the digital world. Judging from attitudes like Lawee's, if an individual is not already at the top, there is little likelihood they'll even have a shot at the bottom of the Google pyramid, not to mention that of its competitors.

There's no doubt that the advertising industry will recover from the recession but, as for its employees, that's another story. The result of a highly-digitized society is that it takes fewer people to keep it running and this is especially true for the world of advertising, which was once dependent on a sea of near-millions and is now making its way to an elite team of several thousand. Just as mail-order catalogs did away with the traveling salesman, software and search engines are eclipsing the advertising executive. In the ashes of a smoldering industry, the flames of technology promise new life. However, in the Digital Age of Advertising, it will be the internet savvy individual, not the advertising executive, who keeps the torch lit.

8
The Entertainment Industry Gives Way to the Intertainment Industry

The influence of the internet on the entertainment industry struck hard and fast in 1999, when a little website called Napster appeared on the scene. Before it knew what hit it, the music industry was in a state of near collapse as word spread like wildfire about this new music sharing program. All you had to do was go online, find your favorite artist, song or album and download it for free. Download speeds were slower back then, but Napster made it possible to make a list of downloads, go to bed and wake up to find a couple of dozen new music releases on your hard drive. After that, it was just a matter of copying them onto a CD or one of those new fangled MP3 players.

Napster turned out to be both a blessing and a curse to the music industry. On the one hand, big names like Metallica became alarmed when they learned their music was being distributed for free online. On the other hand, a lesser known band, Radiohead, finally gained international recognition and sales after 2 million copies of their album were distributed free of charge 3 months before it was released as a CD. The exposure garnered from the pirate copies of their album, *Kid A*, outweighed the lost revenue from those 2 million downloads.

Whether Napster was a boon or a bane to performers ended up being a moot point. The original Napster shut down in 2001 when it was unable to follow the court's directive to monitor its network activities and filed for bankruptcy in 2002. However, the Napster experiment changed the course of music history. From that day forward, digital music was king and consumers expected to get more music for less money. The industry had no choice but to comply.

The motion picture industry was only spared the same fate as the music industry for a short few years, until fiber optic cables and other IT improvements made it possible to download full length movies quickly and reliably. The lesson of Napster was not lost online and the infrastructure for protecting video streaming from piracy was in place by the time it became possible for the average internet user to download full length films, but there was little anyone could do about the public's wholehearted embrace of the internet for its entertainment needs.

How Technology Is Turning Entertainment into 'Intertainment'

Napster was made possible by the MP3 music format. MP3 is the shortened version of an acronym, MPEG3. The MPEG part of the acronym stands for Motion Picture Experts Group with the 3 represents the codec. The history of MP3s goes back to 1987, when a group of researchers at Germany's Fraunhofer Institut began working on ways to compress audio files without losing sound quality. They did this by eliminating imperceptible sounds, thus reducing the size of the file from the 30 to 60 MB on a typical CD down to around 3 MB. Once that was done, technology just had to catch up with it.

The first MP3 player wasn't released until 1998. That was the now long forgotten MPMan. It was Napster that got the ball rolling for the mad rush to develop MP3 players, a market that Apple has dominated since it introduced the first iPod in 2001. The iPod is often held responsible for reviving Apple's fortunes and image after its battering by its operating system arch rival, Microsoft.

Apple followed up the iPod with iTunes. Launched in April of 2003, by June of the same year, Apple iTunes "stores" (online platforms) had already sold 3.5 million songs and sales were already up to half a million per week. By 2010, the number had reached 11.7 billion songs. By then, music downloads were just a portion of iTunes success, albeit a large portion. Also downloaded on iTunes were over 450 million TV episodes and 100 million movies. While these numbers are not large in comparison to the music downloads, iTunes is not the best or most used platform for audio-visual entertainment. There are much bigger players there, and they are changing the face of the motion picture industry forever.

How a Motion Picture Lion Lost its Roar

On November 3, 2010, BBC News reported that MGM Studios had filed for Chapter 11 bankruptcy. This 20th century giant of motion picture entertainment, whose iconic roaring lion is one of the world's most familiar symbols, had lost its roar. As part of the proceedings, Spyglass Entertainment executives were to be given the reins of the company. According to some sources, the bankruptcy proceedings are mainly an attempt to wipe away a $4 billion debt and give the company a fresh start. MGM, a company that has been bought, sold and restructured many times, found its back against the wall when it was unable to service the interest on its debt, primarily because of a decrease in television and DVD sales. Since MGM has produced some of the most popular films in history, including the James Bond series and has a catalog of over 4000 films, there is only one plausible explanation for this lost revenue: people don't watch movies on TV or DVDs anymore; they watch them online.

It's not just MGM that is feeling the pinch from the internet. Other motion picture giants like Disney and Time Warner's Warner Brothers are feeling it, too. According to Bloomberg, DVD sales dropped by a massive 16.5% in the last 9 months of 2010 and they show no signs of slowing down. While the adoption of the newer BluRay technology was given some of the blame, the online figures show what's really going on in the intertainment industry. At the same time DVD sales plummeted in 2010, online spending increased and video-on-demand's share of the pie increased by 20%. While Blockbuster video filed for bankruptcy, Netflix Inc. added 1.93 million subscribers to its list in the final quarter of 2010.

The Netflix Phenomenon

Netflix started out in 1998 as predominantly a DVD mail order company, but from the beginning, this Silicon Valley company had its eye on the internet. It had to wait for technology to catch up with its vision, but now that it has, Netflix is turning out to be a threat even to cable giants like Comcast and Time Warner. How has it done it? Netflix changed its strategy from one of competition to one of innovation and put all its resources into its streaming video service. By 2011, the company had 20 million subscribers and was offering unlimited downloads for a paltry $7.99 per month.

The world still prefers to watch movies and TV series on their large screen TVs. Now that internet connected televisions and related devices are available, it's just a matter of time before streaming content becomes universal. Netflix isn't sitting around waiting for that day to come, though. As they boast on their website:

"Among the large and expanding base of devices streaming from Netflix are Microsoft's Xbox 360, Nintendo's Wii and Sony's PS3 consoles; an array of Blu-ray disc players, Internet-connected TVs, home theater systems, digital video recorders and Internet video players; Apple's iPhone, iPad and iPod touch, as well as Apple TV and Google TV. In all, more than 200 devices that stream from Netflix are available in the U.S."

How the New Intertainment Industry Hurts the Job Market

From the point of view of the consumer, all of these technological advances in how music and movies are being distributed are welcome news. We can, after all, get more entertainment faster and cheaper than ever before. Instead of being slaves to television programming schedules or having to drive to the local video store, we just go online. The iPod and iTunes were not forced onto the public, they were enthusiastically embraced. The same is true of Netflix. What the public doesn't realize, however, is that every new one of these advances in technology costs more jobs than it creates.

In the music industry, recording companies have laid off scores of: engineers, technicians, studio musicians, production workers, executives, salesmen, distribution workers and even their maintenance staffs. Their distribution companies have almost ceased to exist. Retail music outlets have gone out of business and along with them have gone their staff members. Those who have not gone out of business entirely have drastically cut down on staff numbers. The situation is identical in the motion picture industry.

As in so many other sectors of the economy, the biggest losers in the "intertainment" revolution have largely been those at the bottom of the employment heap. Music and motion picture executives who have been able to adapt continue to prosper, as do the superstars of music and the big screen. However, just as online bookselling giant Amazon has forced former retail giants like Borders Books into bankruptcy, online giants like Netflix have forced former heavyweights like Blockbuster into retail oblivion. With the closure of thousands of video stores comes the loss of tens of thousands of jobs. Where those former employees will go to find work is anybody's guess. There are only so many fast food outlets to go around.

9

Lawyers Condemned to Death by the Internet

For generations, a Law degree has been seen as a virtual guarantee of a lucrative income for life. While there has always been a certain amount of myth to this assumption, in the past it has always been true that a reasonably skilled lawyer could expect to make a comfortable income for life and that some lawyers could become very wealthy. This is rapidly changing, though, and lawyers are finding their hard-earned law degrees have little value other than as nicely designed diplomas to hang on their walls. The internet is becoming their judge, jury and executioner as increasingly budget-conscious employers and former clients go online to find cheaper services.

While the legal profession lays the blame for the unprecedented number of unemployed lawyers on the shockwaves from the global recession of 2008-2009, they, like so many other sectors of the economy are overlooking the negative effect the internet is already having on the job market. In late 2010, the official unemployment rate in the United States stood at just over 9%. For lawyers, it topped 10%. Business, professional and news media optimistically predicted a slow return to more normal levels of unemployment, but as the months rolled by, there was little real change. The pundits laid the blame on events in the Middle East and confidently asserted that the "fundamentals" were still sound and things would soon return to "normal." What all of these pundits seem to be blind to is the fact that what used to be "normal" is now as outdated as the horse and buggy, thanks to the internet.

Yes, the recession has taken its toll on the job market, but that is only a small part of the story and masks the true cause the crisis the legal profession is facing. A look at how the internet is affecting a lawyer's chances for employment reveals that even if a miraculous turnaround in the economy does eventuate, they will still be looking for work outside their field of expertise and even if they do find work, they will receive only a fraction of the money attorneys have historically made. In the short term, the winners will be cheaper legal professionals from developing countries, but in the longer term, the only lawyers who will be earning a living wage will be "virtual" online legal services and a handful of corporate and criminal attorneys.

Outsourcing to India

On August 04, 2010, the *New York Times* published an online article titled *Outsourcing to India Draws Western Lawyers*. The thrust of the article was not about the handful of U.S. and British lawyers who were finding employment in India, but about the kind of work they were finding and its implications for the future of the legal profession in Western countries. These lawyers were acting as advisers for teams of Indian lawyers working online for American and British companies and law firms. At the time of writing, the revenue Indian online legal services received was $440 million, up 38% since 2008. The article also noted that this was not just a short term trend, but something to be seriously concerned about. According to Harvard's David B. Wilkins, this is "not a blip. This is a big historical movement." How big? The article estimated that by 2014, outsourcing legal work to India would be a billion dollar business.

In 2006, changes in regulations regarding the storage and maintenance of electronic data for Federal courts were initiated. These changes immediately increased the volume of work available, but there were not enough affordable legal professionals in the U.S. to keep up with the work, so the courts turned to cheaper Indian legal professionals.

This outsourcing of legal work to India piqued the interest of companies and law firms looking for cheaper routine legal work. Then the recession came. Initially, the recession proved to be a boon to some sectors of the legal profession as there was plenty of work to be done processing bankruptcies. However, the recession also meant that businesses everywhere were feeling the financial pinch and were looking for cheaper labor wherever they could find it. Those who needed legal work found that cheaper labor in India.

An article about U.S. firms outsourcing to India in the *New York Times2* begins with the story of a COO who asked outside counsel to customize residential leases. They came back with a price tag of $400,000. He turned down the offer and chose to try an outsourcing firm located in India that did the work for $45,000. Not only did this COO think the work done was of good quality, but he has been working with the Indian firm ever since.

This was back in 2003 and the trend, initially received with skepticism by lawyers, companies and individuals seeking legal advice, has exploded since. Issues regarding the competence of Indian lawyers have been resolved and while outsourcing legal work was previously the exception, it is now becoming the rule. Even large American corporations such as DuPont, Cisco Systems, and Morgan Stanley have legal departments based in India. Why wouldn't they, when they can pay an Indian lawyer as little as $8,160 per year instead of the $150,000 they would have to pay a U.S. attorney? 2

Outsourcing in the Philippines

Another country that is benefiting from outsourcing is the Philippines. Not only does the Philippines share the English language with the U.S., but it has the same type of legal system as well. According to an article in *Bloomberg Businessweek*, the chemical powerhouse DuPont uses lawyers from the Philippines to analyze important legal documents. DuPont anticipates saving 40% to 60% or up to $6 million by having this work done offshore. This may be a small fraction of the $200 million they company spends annually on legal services, but it may just be the beginning. DuPont points out that 70% of what a law firm charges for is paralegal work, which is billed at about $150 an hour. The same work can be accomplished in the Philippines for around $30 an hour. Then there is the added benefit that firms in the Philippines are willing to work a rotating shift and provide services on a 24 hour basis. This is a service no American firm is willing to offer.

Without the internet and related technologies, this outsourcing could not occur. It relies largely on the ability to upload and download files instantaneously. Using cloud computing, these files can be shared online in real time, just as if the Indian or Filipino lawyer was in a nearby office cubicle.

Do it Yourself Law

Another reason for the demise of the lawyer is the plethora of "do-it-yourself" or DIY legal services, such as LegalZoom, NOLO, and the Legal Kit Store. One look at LegalZoom and it is easy to see why many people might give it a try. They have testimonials on the home page, with a long list of services they provide for both personal and business needs. Included in their list of DIY services are Wills, real estate deed transfers, trademarks, copyrights and even corporation dissolutions. Getting this work done involves very little effort and no legal expertise on the client's part. First, you complete a questionnaire. LegalZoom's online team then reviews your questionnaire, completes the paperwork and sends the documents to you for your signature. All of this can be done for as little as $35.00.

The LegalZoom website includes a disclaimer that states it is not a law firm and does not act as a lawyer, but is there only to assist customers in representing themselves. If you have complex legal issues, they suggest you seek the services of an attorney. While there is merit to this suggestion, it is also true that most consumers know that many legal documents do not need the high price tags attorneys put on them.

Nolo is another site that offers DIY forms and online legal services. They offer information and services on well over a dozen different topics, including Accidents and Injury, Bankruptcy, Family Law and even driving related topics.

Legal Kit Store offers DIY legal kits and states that there is no attorney required. They offer kits in bankruptcy, business partnership, divorce & dissolution, quitclaim deeds and many others. The site repeatedly states that a layman can handle many legal matters by himself and save a great deal of money. Most of the documents they offer at the Legal Kit Store are downloadable computer and accessible within minutes.

Websites like LegalZoom, Nolo, and the Legal Kit Store are just three examples of online services that are increasingly making many jobs that were formerly the domain of attorneys redundant. While it can be argued that this is a benefit to consumers, this is of little comfort to an attorney waiting for his phone to ring.

Online Legal Research and Information Services

One of the ways lawyers justify their high fees is by claiming expertise in law. While this argument may have merit, laymen who wish to understand the law can now find the information they need quickly and easily online. Sites such as LexisNexis, while geared towards practicing attorneys, are also accessible to the general public. A search engine allows anyone to look up "free case law" and find State, Federal and Supreme Court documents going back to 1781.

While informational sites like LexisNexis may not encourage laymen to defend themselves in court, they are having a negative impact on the legal profession in other ways. With the ease that lawyers can now find the legal information they need, it is no longer as necessary as it once was for them to employ junior staff to do their research for them. If they do need a trained lawyer, they can outsource the work to India or the Philippines, where an inexpensive lawyer can have access to the same online information an attorney in the United States has.

Time Saving with Videoconferencing

Video conferencing is another reason why lawyers may be unable to find work. Lawyers who use video conferencing are able to work more hours in a day if they use video conferencing because they can save time by not having to drive to meetings in their home town and also save time in airports and while traveling if they leave their near by area. This ability to speak to a person or even depose them via video conferencing can knock off time spent traveling, which in turn means more hours to work on the case, or potentially another case. Whereas it may have taken a firm two lawyers to do this work, it can potentially be narrowed down to one, thus eliminating the need for yet another lawyer in a field that is already being decimated.

The Verdict

Any professional who demands a high fee for his services will only receive remuneration in relation to his expertise and the relative demand for his services. Lawyers are such professionals. In the United States, it takes seven years of education and a difficult bar examination in order to be accepted into the legal profession. After that, a lawyer must work long hours under a great deal of stress in order to achieve success. As long as the promise of a lucrative career and a comfortable retirement lies ahead of him, he is willing to make the necessary sacrifices.

Currently, it is estimated that around 44,000 people graduate from U.S. law schools each year. These are the ones law firms would traditionally hire to work fifty to sixty hours per week doing their routine work and research. In India, an estimated 80,000 graduate from law school each year. Indian graduates are finding better paying jobs with greater chances for advancement working for online companies who give them work outsourced from the United States and Great Britain than Indian law firms are offering. Why would a U.S. law firm invest in a U.S. graduate when he could get an equally qualified Indian graduate for a fraction of the price? A few might do it for sentimental or patriotic reasons, but as in any industry, the bottom line is a law firm's major concern.

Some of those young graduates may try to go into private practice, but the majority will be lucky if they can even find law-related work. What work they do find in their field will usually offer a fraction of what they previously could have expected to make. There is increasingly little incentive for young students to study law as the word gets out that what was once one of the most coveted professions is now simply not worth the effort and expense.

The situation is not likely to improve, either, especially when you consider that many lawyers are finding work supervising and training teams of Indian and Filipino lawyers overseas. One of the main reasons why U.S. lawyers are still in demand is because the companies that hire them do not trust the expertise of overseas trained legal professionals. When this bias is overcome, there will be virtually no need for native born and educated associates whatsoever.

The gavel may have dropped back in 2006, when RR Donnelley acquired OfficeTiger, a business processing outsourcing (BPO) service for $250 million. Now a lawyer with five years experience in the Philippines gladly works for half the salary a paralegal is paid in the United States. Today, OfficeTiger has been fully integrated with RR Donnelley and a full range of outsourced legal work is offered on the Donnelley website. The level of professionalism is undisputed and it is all geared towards offering comprehensive legal services online.

While lawyers in the Philippines and India may now be rejoicing, their days are probably numbered as well. Ultimately, the only lawyers who will be needed will be those few who happen to be needed in court or who are hired to make and define law. This elite group of legal professionals will reap huge financial benefits, while the vast majority of lawyers will be condemned by the internet to employment death.

10
The Demise of the Stock Broker

From 1776, when Adam Smith published The Wealth of Nations until the Great Depression, when the financial edifice came crashing down, the United States based its economic belief system on the assumption that the free enterprise system was virtually fail safe. For a time, Keynesian economics was viewed as a necessary correction to that belief system, but after WWII, when America's world economic dominance renewed our confidence, our faith in the system was restored.

Stock brokers, whose reputations had been tarnished, to say the least, after the Depression, were back in vogue. In the heady years of deregulation and mergers and acquisitions, stock prices soared. Sure, there were hiccoughs along the way, some of them serious, but we bounced back. Maybe those stock brokers who gave investors bad advice along the way suffered some setbacks to their credibility, but their opinions were the only opinions we had to go on. They were the experts, with their fingers on the pulse of market.

When the bubble burst in late 2007, the reputations of stock brokers became tarnished again. According to Forrester Research, fewer than half of respondents to this question responded in the affirmative: "My financial provider does what's best for me, not just its own bottom line."

Many stockbrokers have sidestepped their critics by redefining themselves as "financial advisers" and to some extent, this new title has given them life support, but it's too little, too late.

Their days are numbered and it's not just because of their tarnished reputations. It's because they are not needed. The internet is making stock brokers and "financial advisers" redundant. The "Great Recession" is just hastening their demise.

ECNs (Electronic Communications Networks)

It usually takes a disaster to initiate change in established customs. The stock market is no exception to this rule. Before Black Monday, the 19th of October, 1987, no one really disputed the importance of the stock broker in the exchange between buyers and sellers of stocks and other investment instruments. Love him or hate him, he was the middleman between the two. Then, on Black Monday, something happened. NASDAQ market makers stopped answering their phones. This left retail investors with no one to turn to when they needed someone the most.

As a response to this, when NASDAQ recovered from the shock of Black Monday, it made some adjustments to its system so that retail investors would get priority access over market makers and institutional investors. Using the Small Order Execution System (SOES), they were enabled to instantly initiate trades of 1000 shares or less. They were able to do this electronically. While it was still the brokers who made the trades and the real money, the writing was on the wall: it was just a matter of time before the internet age would make it possible to cut out the middleman, the stock broker, altogether.

Savvy traders, looking for ways to make faster trades and higher profits, took advantage of this new way to get the edge over the institutional investors. One of these, Harvey Houtkin, became known as the first of the "SOES Bandits", as they came to be known. Houtkin was largely responsible for spreading the word about how small traders could beat the big investment firms by using the SOES system.

These SOES traders took it one step further by using their own computer terminals to process their orders using then fledgling Electronic Communications Networks (ECNs), routing them via the internet. Throughout the early nineties, ECNs became increasingly sophisticated; first being able to match trades at increasingly high speeds and then, as the technology improved, being able to scour the rest of the market for matches using what was called a "smart order router."

So far, all of this was working to the advantage of smart stockbrokers who took advantage of ECNs. Their machinations backfired on them, though, when market makers were hit by scandal that showed they were deliberately manipulating the NASDAQ market, NASDAQ implemented new Order Handling Rules that were quickly passed by the SEC. What these rules did was mandate that ECN stock bids and offers be placed alongside those of the NASDAQ order makers. This leveled the playing field and created greater transparency. It also put ECNs on an equal footing with the formerly all powerful market makers.

The playing level was leveled further when, in response to regulatory inequities in the market due to increasingly popular ECNs, the SEC passed Regulation ATS (Alternative Trading Systems) in 1998. This landmark regulation allowed ATSs, specifically ECNs, to choose whether they wished to operate as broker-dealers or exchanges in their own right. The stage was set for the total transformation of the stock market and, ultimately, the demise of the traditional stockbroker.

In the year 2000, the Securities and Exchange Commission published a study titled, Electronic Communications Networks and After-Hours Trading. In its introduction, the study noted that "ECNs currently conduct the vast majority of their trading during the regular trading sessions from 9:30 a.m. to 4:00 p.m., averaging around 3% of share volume in exchange-listed stocks and 30% of the volume in Nasdaq stocks." This was in the year 2000. The numbers have changed dramatically since then. Nonetheless, the electronic age of trading stocks had been duly noted by the SEC. However, these numbers were only of concern to stockbrokers who didn't jump on the ECN bandwagon. At that time, according to the SEC study, ECNs included only "retail investors, institutional investors, market makers, and other broker-dealers." It should have been of concern to all stock brokers, but those were the heady days of the new millennium, when stockbrokers were still the "Masters of the Universe" and the stock market had nowhere to go but up. Then the market came crashing down and with it, the careers of thousands of traditional stockbrokers. A new breed of trader moved in to take their place.

High Frequency Traders

At the time when the SEC published its Special Report on ECNs and after hours trading, there were already nine ECNs in operation. Competition between them became primarily competition for transaction speed. Every hundredth of a second gained in speed gave one ECN the edge over the other. Today, it's the High Frequency Traders (HFTs) who get all the action on what is called Wall Street, but is actually a bank of computers in New Jersey. How much of the action do they get? According to Business Insider, "HFT trading is concentrated at the bigger firms like Goldman Sachs and UBS. The 12 largest brokers are expected to execute 71% of share volume in 2011."

The Tabb Group research firm puts the figure a little more conservatively, saying that "High-frequency traders now account for as much as 60 percent of daily volume." They go on to say that the "most prolific HFT outfits, such as Getco in Chicago, Tradebot Systems in Kansas City, Mo., or RGM Advisors in Austin, Texas, can individually generate as much as 5 percent or 10 percent of all the stocks traded in the U.S. on a given day." The key word there is "individually." Collectively, their clout is massive.

ECNs are the real power now, while Wall Street is really "little more than a theatrical backdrop for cable TV correspondents." Ironically, this quote comes from MSNBCs Bloomberg Business Week. The same source goes on to say that the NYSE took less than 25% of equity traffic in 2010. In 2005, it took 80%. To say the drop has been precipitous would be an understatement.

If ECNs are the movers and shakers on "Wall Street" now and High Frequency Traders are the new breed of "stockbroker", what do they look like? What are their qualifications? Are they really stock brokers at all? Not according to this CNBC article, as cited in Yahoo Finance:

"Indeed, the computer whizzes have become the dominant players on Wall Street. Earlier this year, Getco, among the largest high-frequency firms, became a designated market maker on the floor of the NYSE, a role formerly held by specialists. This summer, the NYSE opened up a massive computer data center in Mahwah, N.J., to cater to high-speed trading firms."

Getco is a perfect example of how the stock market works today and why stock brokers are a doomed breed. A quick glance at Getco's website gives the impression that they are a large team of traders and other financial experts. Globally, the company has over 300 "associates" and are "among the top 5 participants by volume" on at least 11 exchanges. If those associates were stock brokers, they would be very busy indeed, but most of those associates are not stock brokers. At Getco, automation is the name of the game: "Our philosophy is to automate when possible, while preserving the judgment and perspective our Associates bring to our trading and development processes." This is a polite way of saying that Getco's goal is to eliminate as many stock brokers as they possibly can by becoming one computerized digital "stockbroker" without a human face.

Still, there are those, like the Bureau of Labor Statistics, who believe that demand for stock brokers will grow at least through 2018. Then they turn around and contradict themselves with this statement:

"Competition for jobs will continue to be keen with more applicants than available openings. Additionally, the recent financial crisis has resulted in mass consolidation in the financial industry, a scenario that will likely result in fewer positions as companies attempt to streamline operations by eliminating duplicate tasks."

"Mass consolidation" is another understatement. Perhaps the Bureau should take a look at what's happening in the real world. According to a September 2010 article in the Atlantic Monthly with the ominous title, Hiring Freezes and Layoffs Begin on Wall Street, it's near carnage on Wall Street. The Atlantic cites a Bloomberg article by Michael J. Moore that says, "Securities firms around the world will cut as many as 80,000 jobs in the next 18 months."

A Business Insider article about Wall Street layoffs says it more bluntly in a piece with the title, Layoff Carnage is Back On Wall Street. According to this article, eight Wall Street firms are laying off staff at all levels, while many others are imposing hiring freezes. Firms included in the "carnage" are names like Goldman Sachs, Bank of America and JP Morgan, not to mention brokerages like Knight Capital, which was laying off 8% of its staff.

Who Are Getting the Jobs?

Of course, some people are getting jobs, but they're not proprietary traders. The title of this article says it all: JP Morgan

Shutting Down All Prop Trading Desks. This is due to changes in financial regulations and many firms are simply changing the roles and names of prop traders rather than drastically cutting staff. As the article says: "many have been moved to client based desks." Still, according to Bloomberg, Morgan Stanley initiated a hiring freeze in 2010, promising no more layoffs in that year. They didn't mention anything about 2011.

Fixed income traders are not getting the jobs, either. CNBCs NetNet article titled, Get Ready for the Fixed Income Bloodbath quotes a "highly placed Wall Street insider" as saying: "We're easily going to cut a quarter to a half of our traders and back office in fixed income. Everyone else is going to do it too.

According to a *Business Insider* article by Courtney Comstock, *Everyone's Least Favorite Traders Are the Only Ones Getting Hired Right Now*, only High Frequency Traders are being hired. But HFTs are not really stock brokers in name or experience. As the article goes on to say: "Recruiters said Nomura, JPMorgan, Bank of Montreal, Citigroup, Barclay's Capital, Goldman Sachs, and Deutsche Bank are all asking them to find them new hires that are high frequency traders, or in Goldman Sachs' case, quantitative analysts with a Ph.D."

Quantitative analysts with a PhD? What do they know about trading stocks? Probably nothing, but they know plenty about quantitative analysis, which is what today's stock market is really all about. A term that has become almost synonymous with high frequency trading today is algorithmic trading. Those PhDs who are in such demand are the ones who create the algorithms that make smart routers even smarter. Some of the data their algorithms process include the price and liquidity of a security, the timing of an order execution and the costs of transaction. They can split large orders up and trickle them out in waves in order to keep a large buy or sell order off the radar. These are just some of the basic tasks algorithmic traders can carry out and more algorithms are being added all the time.

In high frequency trading, speed is all important. Since the market became decimalized in the year 2000, minute changes in the prices of securities can be taken advantage of by large volume traders, but only if they have the computerized technology necessary to track and follow the changes and the ability to act fast. Clearly, the less people involved in making a trade, the faster the transaction can take place.

Direct Access Trading Systems (DATS) allow traders to trade stocks and other financial instruments with market makers or specialists directly or even initiate immediate order executions. By eliminating the middleman, they save precious seconds or even minutes of time. Where do both small and institutional investors go to get access to DATS? They go online.

Online Brokers, otherwise known as Discount Brokers are the only ones getting jobs today and they aren't really stock brokers at all. This is not a new phenomenon. An April 2005 article in Bloomberg's Business Week titled Death of a Stock Salesman, suggests that it was already happening then, before the "Great Recession." The article, by Amey Stone, cites several reasons for the decline in stock broker's fortunes, one of the major ones being "improvements in technology and the rise of online discount brokerages." Even in 2005, before the recession, discounters were continually driving down their commissions in order to capture more market share.

There may be a smattering of jobs for traditional stock brokers who work for wealthy clients that can afford their higher commissions, but these brokers now prefer to call themselves "financial advisers" to avoid the stigma of the fast talking stockbroker who, like the stereotypical used car salesman, has only a quick profit for himself in mind. The large brokerages don't even want small investors because the commissions are too small, having been eroded by competition from the discount brokers. Therefore, they don't need stock brokers to handle their smaller accounts.

Since the recession, those who still have capital to invest and continue to believe that playing the stock market is a viable way to make money have moved to online "brokerages" in droves. Some of them choose to use a Discount Broker online, but even the terminology there has changed. When you go to an online broker today, you are given a choice between making a "broker assisted" (discount broker) transaction or skipping the broker altogether and buying and selling your own stocks directly.

Thanks to robotic trading platforms, passive trading is increasingly seen as the savviest way to invest. Whether they live up to their claims is a moot point. The important thing is that users believe they do. CoolTrade is an example of this. CoolTrade is affiliated with giants E*Trade, Interactive Brokers, TD Ameritrade, FXCM, MB Trading and Optionshouse. Why pay a traditional stockbroker a $35+ fee when you can get the same service online for $5? Online brokers make compelling arguments for their services and offer options like "broker assisted" trading (discount brokers) for those who want some human assistance. However, by providing software tools and training for traders, these online "brokers" are cutting out the middleman altogether.

CoolTrade vigorously promotes robotic trading. In essence, robotic trading is exactly what it sounds like: a "robotic" software program does everything for you. The investor simply has to set the parameters of the trade and the "Robotic Trader may be set to start by itself in the morning and trade the market all day 100% unattended." For those who like to get involved in their transactions, the CoolTrade "Strategy Wizard" allows you to "rapidly filter through all 8000+ NYSE, NASDAQ and AMEX stocks for only those that meet your investment criteria." The trademarked "CoolTrade Intelligent Trading System" Strategy Wizard also includes sample investment strategies, downloadable strategies from other successful CoolTrade subscribers and other tools that make the average investor feel like he has dozens of top Wall Street advisers at his beck and call, 24 hours a day.

TradeKing is another online broker that actively promotes cutting out the middle man, saying, "The foremost benefit of acting as your own stock broker is that it allows you to minimize the transaction costs associated with each trade." TradeKing is no small-fry in the online brokerage business, either. It is jointly owned by Dow Jones & Company, Inc. and Hearst Publications.

E*Trade is often cited as being the most advanced online brokerages. The company is certainly one of the largest and oldest, having been in operation for over 20 years. E*Trade covers everything, including stocks, ETFs, bonds and even banking. It boasted over 2.3 million subscribers and almost $150 billion in worldwide customer assets in October, 2009. The E*Trade platform includes training tools, robotic trading and everything else an investor needs. While they don't come right out and say it on their homepage, the implications are clear: Why use a broker when you can do it better, faster and smarter yourself?

While E*Trade remains consistently at or near the top of the heap of online trading platforms, it is by no means without competition. Smart Money's 2010 Broker Survey put E*Trade's arch rival Fidelity in the top spot after having been second to E*Trade the previous three years. The reason for the switch was largely because Fidelity's commissions and fees are among the lowest in the industry. The discount wars between the players in the online brokerages are fierce because cheap commissions and fees are what subscribers are looking for the most. When Fidelity was threatened by Charles Schwab, who slashed their commissions a full 30% to $8.95 per trade, Fidelity countered with a $7.95 commission and anchored its position at the top. In contrast, Bank of America's online arm, Banc of America charges up to $14 per trade unless you keep at least $25,000 in their bank. It's little wonder that Banc of America finished dead last in Smart Money's survey.

Fees and commissions aren't the only determinants of a trading platform's popularity, though. Part of the reason for a company's high ranking is its record of customer service. The top online trading platform for customer service in the 2010 survey was TradeKing. This wasn't enough for them to beat out Fidelity, though, partly because Fidelity's trading tools were considered second to none. Their mobile apps, an increasingly in demand tool and one that online brokers are spending huge amounts of money to develop, were cited as the best, as were their other tools, like stock screening and streaming quotes. Transaction speed, too, is of vital importance to traders. Here, too, Fidelity excelled, with an average of just four seconds between sign-in and transactions completion. While a competitor's 16 second trade might sound reasonably fast to an outsider, it was considered positively glacial by users in comparison - and completely unacceptable.

With platforms like E*Trade, Charles Schwab (who boasted client assets of over $1.5 trillion as of November 30, 2010) and the other big online brokers, even stock brokers who have changed their label to "financial adviser" are under threat, since you can make virtually any financial transaction through them and even customize your long term financial strategies. Subscribers can open retirement accounts, rollover their 401(k), transfer existing IRAs and automate their retirement investments. The top online services even include full banking services that allow you to set up bank accounts, get low interest 30 year fixed rate mortgages and home equity loans online. All of these things can be done at rates so low, no individual financial planner could possibly compete against them.

Those stock brokers still clinging to the idea that there is a job market out there somewhere for them would be excused for thinking that a company like E*Trade would have at least a few openings in their brokerage division. On January 12, 2011, a quick look at their Careers page produced this discouraging result under their Brokerage job listings: "There are currently no opportunities in this area." The same was true of Investment Management. However, there were 48 available jobs in Information Technology on the same date.

In response to customer demand, the big players in online financial services have been opening brick and mortar customer service centers. However, you are not likely to find teams of stock brokers sitting behind their desks waiting to give you their sage advice. What their customers want most is advice about how to invest online and practical seminars for "self-managed" investors. If a broker's advice is needed, that can be done online, but at a substantially higher commission and fee.

One online source that had some openings for stockbrokers was JobSearchUSA.com, a popular job search engine that lists tens of thousands of job openings. On January 14, 2011, they listed a whopping 12 openings for stock brokers. Two of these were in New York, while the rest were in a smattering of other states, including Florida, Utah, Texas, and Alaska. All of these jobs were listed by

Scottrade, another one of the big online discount brokers. Scottrade has been aggressively opening branches throughout the country in an effort to capture a larger share of the investor market.

At the end of 2010, Scottrade celebrated the opening of its 500th branch office. CEO and company founder, Rodger Riney appeared on CNBC's Squawk on the Street in order to explain why he felt in-person help was still important to the "self-directed investor" (like "self-managed investor", another euphemism for an investor who doesn't want to bother with a stock broker). CNBC's Mark Haines questioned Riney about the company's decision to continue opening brick and mortar branches, asking him if it was because people still liked the "security blanket" of face-to-face interaction with a broker. Riney responded by saying that "branches are coming in very handy for customer education" about "how to use the internet."

If that's the purpose of Scottrade's branch offices, why do they need any stock brokers at all? A look at the jobs listings on their website gives a clue. Those same 12 jobs for stockbrokers were listed on their Careers pages, but they had no openings for Certified Investment Management Consultants (CIMC) or Registered Investment Advisers (RIA), two fields many stock brokers have branched out into in efforts to save their careers. There were 48 job listings for Information Technology experts, though and 55 career opportunities for interns. The job description for these interns included "working side by side with a successful branch manager and experienced stock broker." The stock broker's role at Scottrade is not to trade stocks or consult clients, but to teach a new generation the language of his former trade, in the process making himself redundant.

Generations X and Y

Investment News, "the leading news source for financial advisers" devoted a story to the new generations of potential investors in a January 16, 2011 article, Reaching Out to Generation X and Y Investors. The article, while attempting to remain upbeat about the futures of financial advisers, makes it clear that Generation X (34 to 45 years of age) and Generation Y (16 to 33) are going to be a hard sell. They quote a study conducted by MFS Investment Management by Research Collaborative that concluded: "Gen X/Y doesn't show strong confidence as investors. They seem scared of equities, confused about government bonds, more focused on income and have increased their debt."

Moreover, according to another source cited in the same article, "Gen Y grew up joyriding on the information superhighway ... [and] is skeptical of paying for [a financial] education since many are unemployed after borrowing their way through school."

While Generation X straddles the internet and pre-internet eras, Generation Y has grown up with the internet and trusts it more than it trusts traditional sources of information "because they can Google information or go to Yahoo Finance or Morningstar [Inc.]. They want more evidence-based information, and not necessarily the [traditional adviser-client] face-to-face relationship."

The conclusion drawn by this article was that if financial institutions are going to survive into the next generation, they are going to do so online. This may help explain why Scottrade, a thirty year old company still run by its founder is the only online brokerage so aggressively starting up brick and mortar businesses.

What if the Recession Ends?

While politicians and pundits argue about the best way to solve America's and the world's financial problems, no one really believes that the "Great Recession" is over or that we will be returning to the heady days of the past anytime soon. In fact, many financial soothsayers are predicting even worse times to come. Be that as it may, will an end to the recession bring investors back to stock brokers again? Clearly not, since those investors who remain are a part of a new generation that is comfortable with the internet and trusts it as a source of information. What will happen if the recession ends is that even more investors will open accounts online and become "self managed investors" while the Baby Boomers who supported stock brokers so generously in the past will nurse their existing portfolios in an attempt to live comfortable retirement years. They, too, will use the internet, because they can no longer afford to pay a stockbroker's fees. In the future, the only place where the word "stockbroker" is going to appear will be on an internet search engine and that will only be until a new word, phrase or acronym is found to take its place.

The Paul Bunyans of Wall Street

Perhaps Amey Stone put it best in her Bloomberg article, Death *of a Stock Salesman*:

"Here's a riddle for the 21st century investor: What is the difference between a stockbroker and a financial adviser? Answer: What's a stockbroker?"

What she was missing, though, is that the same question can be asked about financial advisers of all persuasions. The internet and the recession have combined to make financial middlemen of all descriptions obsolete. In Life After Wall Street, writer Mark Koba tries to find where all of those Wall Street layoffs are going to find jobs, since New York City's Independent Budget Office estimated that over 82,000 jobs would be lost in the "finance capital of the world" between 2008 and 2011. While a few career counselors insist that there are jobs available, even they concede that they "aren't necessarily on Wall Street." They aren't "necessarily" in financial services, either. Koba quotes Execu/Search's Ed Fleischman: "There are more openings in health services than in our financial recruiting," he says. He goes on to say, "We were built for financial but have expanded." Reading between the lines, it is clear that even a company whose job is to find jobs for stock brokers and other financial professionals doesn't see a future in the industry.

In one version of the tale of Paul Bunyan, the world's greatest lumberjack finally loses a tree cutting contest to a chainsaw wielding rival. Finally defeated, the dejected giant walks into the woods with his faithful blue ox, Babe, never to be seen again. The Paul Bunyan story was a parable about the end of the frontier era and the beginning of the Industrial Age. Now that the Internet Age is upon us, perhaps another myth will arise. This one will be about one of the giants of Wall Street, finally outsmarted by an online robotic trader. In the final scene, he will be spotted heading for South America, where his shrinking dollars will keep him afloat a little longer. Really, for stock brokers today, it looks like there is nowhere else to go.

11

The Banking Industry Banking on Technology, Eliminating Jobs

For better or for worse, the banking industry is at the heart of the world's economic structures. As became abundantly clear in 2007, how those who control the world's currencies operate their businesses can make or break a nation. The global recession brought this message home to the general public, but a quiet revolution has been occurring in the banking industry for over half a century that has gone largely unnoticed. As banks and other financial institutions have turned to technology, there has been a steady erosion of jobs in the banking sector. Now that the internet has begun to dominate as our principle means of banking, it is almost a certainty that banks as we know them will cease to exist and with them, hundreds of thousands more jobs.

The Creeping Influence of Technology in the Banking Sector

The technological changes that have revolutionized banking are so recent; they are remembered vividly by many bank executives. Charlie E. Walsh, now President and CEO of Farmers and Merchant Bank and Trust, who started out in the bank's Burlington, Iowa branch, is one such executive. Walsh remembers well when he started working at the bank and instead of a desktop computer, he had a desktop ledger. That was in 1969, just when the industry was on the cusp of change.

It wasn't long before computers came on the scene. In those days, the computers were large, taking up so much space they had to be housed in separate rooms. Back then, most everything was still done manually and teams of employees were needed to do everything from painstakingly writing entries in ledgers to making phone calls to find out if checks from other banks had been cleared. The early computers were used primarily for record keeping and number crunching.

ATMs

The first big technological change to ultimately affect the job market in the banking sector came in the 1970s, when Automatic Teller Machines (ATMs) were introduced. At first, bank tellers were probably relieved, since the new fangled machines relieved them of the tedious chore of dealing with $20 withdrawals. They couldn't have known that these machines would eventually relieve them not only of unwanted tasks, but of their very jobs. Introducing ATMs and educating the public about them was a relatively slow process. It wasn't until the late 1980s that their presence became ubiquitous and banks and S&Ls realized they could save significant amounts of money by opening fewer new branches, making them smaller and installing more ATMs, not only outside of the banks themselves but in convenient locations in shopping centers and other high traffic areas where consumers needed access to cash. While these changes did not initially cost jobs, they certainly did not create jobs.

In fact, ATMs were not given the blame as the primary reason for the precipitous job losses in the banking sector during the early 1990s. During that era of mergers and acquisitions, deregulation and other dramatic structural changes, it was restructuring that was held responsible. However, when the banks were given their new found freedom, they realized they could take advantage of ATMs to reduce staff levels.

Electronic Funds Transfer

The 21st century brought new improvements in technology - primarily internet technology. According to an article in the Academic Leadership Online Journal (Winter 2011), we are in the midst of a "third wave of revolution" following the industrial revolution and the agricultural revolution. Dubbed the "electronic revolution", one of the sectors of the economy most affected is the banking sector. As the author, Igwe Stanley Chinedu, states: "For the banking sector, the internet marks the transition from the brick and mortar stage of banking to the branchless stage." He goes on to say: "The growing popularity of Electronic Funds Transfer (EFT) for online bill payment, for instance, is paving the way for a paperless universe where cheques, stamps, envelopes, and paper bills will become obsolete." Along with their obsolescence inevitably comes the obsolescence of once necessary jobs.

Online Banking

As recently as 2006, academic studies of the likely effect of the internet on a bank's profits indicated that increased expenditure on IT and online services could actually be more costly than profitable. According to a white paper by Shirley J. Ho and Sushanta K. Mallick titled, *The Impact of Information Technology on the Banking Industry: Theory and Empirics*, their "empirical study on the panel data of US banks shows that due to severe competition, each bank has over-invested in IT equipment, while the benefits from networks and cost reductions are competed away." The authors did not attempt to offer a solution to the problem, possibly because there was none. By 2006, information technology had been completely integrated into the banking system.

Ho and Mallick concluded their article by saying that under ideal circumstances, when not facing a high network effect (network effect being the growth of traffic or users or the mass adoption of a system), "IT expenditures are likely to (1) reduce payroll expenses, (2) increase market share, and (3) increase revenue and profit." They went on to say that in the US, "although banks use IT to improve competitive advantage, the net effect is not as positive as normally expected." The cruel irony of their conclusion is that while banks took advantage of the technological revolution in order to relieve themselves of the burden of "payroll expenses" (employees), they may have ultimately done so at their own expense.

Whether the banks took the profit-loss implications of online banking into consideration when they expanded their online services in the first decade of the 21st century or not, they had little choice. By then, a society accustomed to the internet demanded online banking services and those banks that lagged behind in offering them faced virtual bankruptcy. By 2009, internet banking had become the preferred method of banking by 25% of the public, with 21%, largely those over the age of 55, preferring to go to their local branch. Another 17% preferred using ATMs to any other form of banking.

The primary reason why people prefer internet banking is because it is easy. When you log on to your online account, you can:

1. Access your account information 24 hours a day
2. Instantly pay your bills, including utility bills, credit cards and other monthly bills
3. Review all of your account transactions

While many consumers initially viewed all of these advantages with trepidation and fears of internet hackers accessing and depleting their accounts, increased security measures, consumer education and the low incidence of online theft gradually reduced those fears. Today, instead of wanting to limit their online banking services, consumers are demanding more and the banks have no choice but to comply.

A recent example of a bank extending its online services and reducing its brick and mortar services is Bank of America. This American institution was a late comer to internet banking and suffered for it when newer banks such as HSBC arrived on the scene. On February 10, 2011, Bloomberg reported that Bank of America, overburdened with non-productive retail branches, was going to close an undisclosed number of them and turn others into Merrill Lynch investment advice centers. This will not result in a jobs-for-jobs trade off, though, because instead of being manned by investment advisors, these re-jigged branches will offer investment advice via remote video conferencing.

According to Bank of America's Chief Operating Manager, Brian T. Moynihan, "We've reduced the opening number, and the closure number has been fairly constant, so over time I think the number will keep going down," He went on to say: "It's not only because of economic changes; there will be leases that come up on buildings that just aren't worth it anymore and we would leave a site." In other words, the bank's strategy for the future is to downsize its retail footprint and enlarge its electronic footprint.

Bank of America is not the only bank that is doing this. According to the same Bloomberg article, US banks "may close as many as 5000 branches through 2012." Additionally, the trend towards transforming existing banks into "specialty stores" will include making those that don't include video conferencing facilities "ATM only" outlets.

The Evolution of Online Banking Services

The example of Bank of America above represents only one type of online banking service. Sometimes referred to as "brick to click" banking, it is an example of an established physical bank offering online services as an adjunct to its retail services. As a rule, bank customers are offered the online services after they have gone into a branch office and signed up for an account in person. Depending on the bank, the online services offered can be limited to basic services such as balance checking, transferring money between accounts within the same bank and paying bills or they can be far more extensive and include related banking services like applying for loans or even opting into an online investment service.

While "brick to click" banking erodes jobs, the other type of online banking service initially creates only IT specialist jobs and ultimately eliminates many of those. Virtual banks, or "direct banks" have no branch offices whatsoever and offer customers significant savings because of their lack of overheads. The first direct bank to be insured by the Federal Deposit Insurance Corporation (FDIC), Security First Network Bank (SFNB), was established in 1995. Three years later, it was taken over by the Royal Bank of Canada. Although this initial venture into direct internet banking was not wildly successful, it was not unsuccessful, either and it demonstrated that the concept of direct banking could work.

It takes any new technology time to be adopted by the general public. The telephone took 50 years before it was universally accepted. The next big technological breakthrough, the television, took half that time and cell phones and PCs only half the time of that. The internet took only 7 years to be universally accepted. This trend towards increasingly rapid diffusion of technology to the masses can partly be attributed to public acceptance of electronics and partly to the technologies themselves. In the case of the internet, for instance, the low cost PC, which had already achieved acceptance, needed only to be connected to a phone line and then an internet service provider took care of the technicalities. Then it was just a matter of making it easier for the average person to go online and giving them an incentive to do so.

When businesses realized the potential of the internet, they pulled out all the stops in order to find out how to provide consumers with the incentive to go online and make use of their products. They learned that there were four main reasons why consumers were attracted to the internet:

* They felt they were in control.
* They felt better informed
* They got better deals
* They were saving money
* They got better solutions

ING Direct is one example of a direct bank that got the customer satisfaction mix right. Founded in 1997, ING Direct Canada, part of the ING group, was the first of the group's forays into direct banking. After three years in operation in Canada, ING United States was established in 2000. Now there are ING Direct services in nine countries. The bank focused from the beginning on giving online customers what they wanted. By giving them services to choose from, they gave customers a feeling of control. By giving them all the information they needed in an easy to use platform, they made them feel informed. They got better deals and saved money because ING Direct passed some of the savings associated with not being burdened with branch offices and staff on to the consumer. All of these added up to better solutions for consumers. In 2009, ING Direct Canada had 1.6 million Canadian customers. These 1,600,000 customers' banking needs were serviced by just 900 employees.

HSBC Direct is an example of how once an innovation takes hold, its adoption increases exponentially. HSBC Direct was launched in the United States in 2005. It now boasts that it is "the world's bank." In 2007, previous to the recession, HSBC was the most profitable bank in the world, with over $19 billion in profits, compared to runner up Bank of America's profits of just under $15 billion. These profits included all of HSBCs operations, including internet, phone banking, retail outlets and investment services.

HSBC is now a gigantic global business, with over 6000 offices in 87 countries worldwide. Its total staff of over 300,000 services 128 million customers worldwide. On average, this means that the company has one staff member for every 427 customers. While it is a large number of employees, they are spread out throughout the world and HSBC has embraced modern technology not only with its direct banking services but by outsourcing and offshoring as much work as possible. Data processing, software engineering and even its customer service operations are headquartered in India (4 locations), Brazil, China and Malaysia. In 2005, Allen Jebson, HSBC's Chief Operating Officer, enthusiastically remarked that in spite of the cost of setting up offshoring operations, "every job moved saves the company $20,000."

Outsourcing and Offshoring

Banks have undergone another round of restructuring since the Great Recession of 2007-2008. By July, 2008, over 121,000 jobs were lost in the banking sector and there have been more since then, even though government bailouts gave banks a new lease on life and they actually started boasting record profits in 2010. The reason, though unstated, is simple: they have been able to shed jobs because technology has made it possible for them to do so. Outsourcing is a popular target for the blame for this, but as the National Outsourcing Association says in its defense, "underlying IT changes and process changes that allow businesses to use less people" are the real culprit.As an advocate of outsourcing, Nigel Roxburgh, the research director for the Association who made that statement, may have glossed over the important point that IT is primarily what allows outsourcing to occur. From his and the banks' point of view, outsourcing is a positive development because, "outsourcing creates a service at a cheaper level and so increases the size of the market for that service."

Whether you want to point the finger at IT or outsourcing is a moot point. They go together hand-in-hand. In the banking sector in particular, without the speed and efficiency of information (internet) technology, outsourcing would not be a viable alternative to hiring domestic labor.

Outsourcing reached fever pitch when the recession hit. As banks and other financial institutions looked for ways to survive, they found it in shipping jobs overseas to countries like India, Pakistan and the Philippines, where there were large numbers of college educated, English speaking, tech savvy workers who were willing and able to work for far less than their Western counterparts would or could. A June 2008 article on the silicon.com website titled, *Credit crunch boosts outsourcing*, quotes Fiona Czerniawska of Management Consultancies Association (MCA), author of a survey of top international banking officials. After questioning them about their views about outsourcing and their plans for the future, she came to this conclusion: "While innovation and creativity is exciting, the credit crunch has also created something of a wake-up call to the financial services sector. Many institutions which have so far ignored the benefits of outsourcing are being forced to revisit it because of financial constraints and liquidity problems."

Those in favor of outsourcing like to tiptoe around the job implications surrounding the practice, but according to Forrester Research as quoted in Yahoo's Associated Content, it is estimated that around 3.3 million white collar jobs and more than $136 billion in wages would shift from USA to other lower cost countries by 2015. They didn't specify how many of those jobs would be banking sector positions, but did mention that it was "especially in Banking Industry" (sic).

Offshoring is a cousin to outsourcing, the difference being that banks and other institutions are the owners of the foreign companies they use to do their work. Offshore companies can be structured in such a way that they can provide a range of services that can drastically erode the work force in their home country, not only within their company, but by offering outsourcing services to other US companies. For example, a software engineering company set up in Hyderabad by one bank or other institution can offer its services to a range of smaller US or European companies, thus increasing its profits while eliminating job opportunities for IT professionals in the United States and Europe. What's more, as trade unions have argued, because these overseas professionals are so much cheaper they their domestic counterparts, wages become suppressed in countries where the cost of living is much higher.

Ironically, offshoring has created so many jobs overseas that wages in those countries are increasing. As a result, the cost savings to companies in 2010 was only 27%, down from 38% in 2001. This isn't stopping companies from increasingly adopting the practice, though. According to one survey, over half the companies included in the survey were planning on increasing their offshore operations.

Mobile Banking: The Final Blow?

There is a prevailing misconception that the US is the first country to adopt new technologies and use them enmasse. This is not always the case and as the ING Direct experiment in Canada shows, has not been the case in internet banking. The United States has also lagged behind the rest of the world in the adoption of mobile technology. When text messaging was just starting to catch on in the US and UK, mobile phone users in the Philippines were already sending 188 text messages per month.

Mobile technology got off to a rocky start. It arrived on the scene with a bang when the new Wireless Access Protocol (WAP) was introduced in the late nineties. WAP was going to make the wired internet redundant. However, WAP technology failed to satisfy the basic needs of consumers and died a quick death at the same time the dotcom bubble burst.

Then came the latest generation of "mobile phones" such as Apple's iPhone and Google's Android. These devices have everything the old protocol lacked. They are easy to navigate, have large enough screens to make viewing easy and can be enhanced simply by downloading applications ("apps"). Some of those apps are for internet banking and related services. The adoption rate of these mobile devices has been phenomenal and is just in its infancy.

Westpac, Bank of America and Chase are three major banks that have apps for iPhone that allow users to integrate their online banking services with their iPhones. Included in the app is a Google map that enables users to find the nearest ATM. This, however, is just the tip of the iceberg. Mobile devices are increasingly being used to make purchases and pay bills without going through the intermediary of a bank. In Korea, the use of "T-Money" has become common. T-Money™ is "electronic cash" stored in the device's sim card. South Koreans use it to pay for public transportation, buy snacks and make small purchases directly from their mobile device. In Japan, too, making purchases via a mobile device has become commonplace. The Bank of Japan estimated that in 2009, "mobile money" was responsible for nearly 3% of all "cash" transactions in that country.

Bankless Mobile Shopping

The United States has lagged behind in using this type of mobile application, but it is now catching on. However, the success of a "cashless" revolution is not dependent on the United States. Mobile money is catching on everywhere in the world, including some of the most unlikely developing countries, such as Kenya, where 70% of the population does not have a bank account. The M-PESA system has been adopted by over 2 million Kenyans, who use it to buy common commodities such as cooking oil and flour. The system of payment is so popular, small businesses who use it often have customers lining up outside of their stores in the morning before they have even opened.

The adoption of systems such as M-PESA and G-CASH, a similar system popular in the Philippines, is increasingly being viewed as a threat to banks. Banks have traditionally shut the world's poor out of the system, seeing them as unprofitable. However, collectively, the world's poor are very wealthy. When they pool their resources into these systems, the transactions that take place already add up to the billions of dollars annually and their adoption is accelerating at a breakneck pace. As a defensive measure, the Bank of the Philippine Islands has joined forces with Globe Telecom and launched a mobile microfinance company, Philipinas Saving Bank Institute (PSBI).

The Downside to Internet Banking

Increasingly, the internet and related technologies are replacing the banking system as we know it. This is seen as a positive development both by banking institutions and consumers. The banks see IT as an opportunity to decrease overheads and increase profits and consumers see online banking as a convenience. In developing countries, internet bank transfers and cashless transactions are seen as a godsend by the world's poor. Aside from systems like M-PESA and G-CASH, billions of dollars are transferred from relatives in developed countries to their families in the rice fields of Cambodia and other third world countries via the internet every year.

While on the surface, there doesn't seem to be a downside to the rapid escalation of the use of the internet in the transferring and monitoring of money, the inevitable result is the elimination of jobs and the transference of wealth to an increasingly smaller percentage of the population. In the United States, the majority of the population still seems to believe they are part of a system that is designed to help the average person. The fact is, the banking system is a business sector, not a community service and its aim is to reduce overheads and increase profits by whatever means possible. In the internet age, going online and eliminating jobs not only makes good business sense, it is what the customer wants.

The public hasn't noticed the effect the internet has had and will continue to have on our livelihoods for two primary reasons. First, the recession led to such a precipitous drop in employment, the impact of the internet has been overlooked. Secondly, in the banking and other sectors, the erosion of jobs due to the internet has been incremental. As the example of Bank of America shows, bank closures are taking place at a measured pace. The loss of 5000 jobs spread out among 50 states and dozens of communities in a single year is noteworthy only in affected communities. Even then, it is viewed as fallout from the recession. What the people don't realize is the fact that their jobs are being systematically destroyed and won't be coming back.

While the pace is "measured", it is likely to increase in speed. As indicated earlier, the embrace of new technologies is accelerating. With it is coming a more rapid acceleration in job losses. While the future is always uncertain, it's a good bet that embarking on a career in the banking sector is not a wise career decision. Perhaps plumbing would be a better bet. Pipes are always breaking and someone will always be needed to fix them.

12

Breaking the Curse of the Internet

Throughout our analysis of the various sectors of the economy and the negative effect the internet is having on the employment situation in America and throughout the world, we have taken a relatively conservative stance. Without having a crystal ball to foresee the future, we have demonstrated that we are facing a job crisis even if an economic recovery takes place. That is the best case scenario and even that has devastating consequences for the average wage earner. As events continue to unfold, it is becoming increasingly clear that the worst case scenario - economic collapse - is the most likely scenario. When that is going to occur, no one can say for certain, but it is in all our interests to prepare for the worst rather than hope for the best. In our view, there are events that may hinder any kind of recovery in the future. The Occupy Wall Street movement is gaining ground. It is not inconceivable that this movement lead to a civil war within the US. At the same time, a debate is raging on about the Super Committee's task to lower the deficit. Based on the latest reports, before this book goes to print, the Super Committee is certain to fail to reach an agreement. Some predict this could lead to the crash of the market, though the rationale offered appears faulty. The Europeans and in particular Italy, Spain and Greece seems to be heading into bankruptcy. With that, the future of Eurozone and the American Banking system has come under question. At the same time there is sable rattling in the Middle East as Israel threatens to bomb Iran. Any of these events may derail any recovery, if there was any, and in the process destroy even more jobs.

In the course of doing research for The Curse of the Internet, as we sifted through the available data online, we deliberately chose to leave out the opinions of "fringe" or "alternative" financial and political analysts. We did this going on the assumption that while the mainstream media and our public officials may bend the facts in order to present an argument, they do not deliberately misinform the public and they have the public interest at heart. The alternative point of view is that the economic recovery is a complete fabrication and that the steps that have been taken (such as QE1 and QE2) are simply desperate steps taken in order to stave off the inevitable collapse of the dollar and breakdown of the American way of life as we have known it.

The frightening thing we learned as we conducted our research is that the alternative analysts seem to be more accurate in their assessment of the current global situation than their mainstream counterparts. Take for example the official unemployment statistics versus the alternative unemployment figures: in February of 2011, the Bureau of Labor Statistics enthusiastically reported that unemployment in America was down to 8.9% - a solid sign that a recovery was taking place. In March, the European Union Times published an article titled, "Real U.S. unemployment rate may be 22.1 percent for February." It sounded like an outlandish claim until you read the article.

The EU Times based its article on information published on John Williams' Shadow Government Statistics website. According to Williams and others, the BLS changed its methodology in 1994, redefining "unemployed" by taking "long-term discouraged workers" who had simply given up looking for jobs off of the roster of the unemployed. Moreover, the BLS has an alternative measure of unemployment known as "U6 unemployment" that includes those who are marginally employed or in part-time employment because they cannot find full-time work. These workers, too, were left out of the BLS's publicly released "U3 unemployment" statistics, though they were included in the "fine print" in its more detailed statistics. In February of 2011, U6 unemployment was 16.7%.

By including the U6 unemployment rate and the numbers of long-term discouraged workers in his statistical analysis, John Williams concluded that the real unemployment rate in the United States was as high as 22.1% in February 2011. Even if you dispute this claim, there is no denying that the Bureau of Labor Statistics and, by extension, the US government and the Federal Reserve Bank have changed the rules to suit their agenda. While Ben Bernanke talks about heading for a more historically sustainable 6% unemployment rate, he is using statistical references that changed in 1994. In other words, what was an unemployment rate of 6% before 1994 is not the same rate that we would get today. Hence, whatever numbers we are given, they are historically irrelevant.

The Other Curse of the Internet

In March of 2011, in a speech before the Senate Foreign Relations Committee, Secretary of State Hillary Clinton said, "America is facing an information war ... and we are losing that war." She went on to point out several online alternative news sources, including China's CCTV, Russia's RT and Al Jazeera. She had good reason to worry. As Global Research TV, a Canadian based alternative news outlet said in its coverage of the speech: "RT's presence on YouTube is a real hit: almost 300 million views, when CNN International is struggling to reach 3 million."

Hillary Clinton's concerns may have been at least partially sparked by the sudden, largely peaceful and completely unexpected overthrow of the Mubarak regime in Egypt. While they stopped short of saying the internet was entirely responsible for galvanizing the people of Egypt, a February 11 article on the Wired website, "Social Media Sparked, Accelerated Egypt's Revolutionary Fire" argued that Facebook and Twitter "did speed up the process by helping to organize the revolutionaries, transmit their message to the world and galvanize international support."

Regardless of their system of government, when people are out of work, hungry and overburdened with debt, they rebel. As this is being written, protests are taking place in Spain and Greece, two of the countries hardest hit by the global recession. The United States may not have reached the tipping point yet, but signs of unrest are apparent throughout the country. In February, 2011, as many as 70,000 ordinary citizens in Madison, Wisconsin gathered to protest Governor Scott Walker's proposal to strip collective bargaining rights as part of his attempt to salvage the Wisconsin economy. This was the largest rally in Wisconsin since the Vietnam War.

The protests were not limited to the State of Wisconsin, either. Union members throughout the country, including teachers, civil service workers and police felt threatened by Governor Walker's proposal. At a "Save the American Dream" rally in New York, several thousand showed up in support of the Wisconsin demonstrators. At that rally, held outside New York's City Hall, speaker John Cody of the Civilian Complaint Review Board, said, "Egypt is inspiring Americans and labor movements" and that "unions need to show acts of solidarity not only across the United States, but across the world." He didn't need to mention how labor unions could demonstrate these global "acts of solidarity": the internet was the obvious and proven medium.

How can the internet be a curse if it has such potential to affect social change, allows us access to a vastly broader spectrum of opinion and gives us the opportunity to actively take part in dialogs and activities that span the globe? There are at least two reasons:

Speed: Social upheavals in Egypt, Libya, Tunisia and elsewhere took place so fast, they lacked any cohesion other than a collective desire to bring about change. What is missing from these movements is a vision for the future or responsible leadership. This is in contrast to the American Revolution. While there were many galvanizing events that occurred, some of them spontaneously, there was time for a workable, acceptable alternative to British rule to be established. The result was the Declaration of Independence, the Constitution and the Bill of Rights.

Sentiment: In the financial arena, the first decade of the 21st century has been described as the "Bubble Decade." In its one hour special by the same name, CNBC highlighted the 3 major bubbles and bursts of the new millennium: the Dotcom Bubble, the Real Estate Bubble and the Private Equity Bubble. While it would be absurd to lay the blame for these bubbles squarely on the shoulders of the internet, it is not far fetched to note the connection between their occurrence and the meteoric rise of the internet.

The obvious relationship between the Dotcom Bubble and the internet aside, the speed and fervour of the buying frenzy that occurred can only be ascribed to the internet. There was no time for reflection: you either got in fast or missed out.

In a Time article that makes fascinating reading in retrospect, journalist Bill Tancer asked on February 27, 2007, "Will The Housing Bubble Burst in 2007?" He believed that the questions internet browsers were asking search engines would be a good indicator of whether or not it would burst. Tanzer recommended readers to "keep an eye on" search terms such as 'sell my house fast,' and 'how to stop a foreclosure' in order to gauge whether or not a crash in real estate values was imminent. His reasoning was that "browsing patterns provide a window into the minds of buyers and sellers and offer more than a glimpse of their feelings about the current market."

What Tanzer was talking about was "market sentiment." As much as we like to believe we are a rational society, history indicates otherwise. As he pointed out, internet browsing patterns can be like a crystal ball, foretelling the future by judging sentiments because market or political sentiments, rational or otherwise, affect the future: they are in a sense self fulfilling prophecies. What is the crystal ball of the internet telling us today?

*Global Research is an alternative news outlet based in Canada that is scathingly critical of U.S. foreign policy. Its parent website, global research.ca, receives over 90,000 visitors per day.

* Max Keiser, a former Wall Street stock broker, hosts a popular show on the English language Russian television station RTV. His U.S. based website, maxkeiser.com receives in excess of 60,000 unique visitors per day.

* Common Dreams, a U.S. based site founded in 1997, publishes well-researched articles scathingly critical of US foreign and domestic policy. Common Dreams receives over 60,000 unique visitors per day.

* David Icke is a former U.K. soccer commentator who became the object of ridicule when he had the "revelation" that the world was being controlled by Reptilian aliens from outer space. His davidicke. com/headlines pages, which grabs headlines from hundreds of sources to support his theories, is read by over 100,000 people daily.

* Alex Jones' Prison Planet, which, like David Icke, focuses on

conspiracy theories, but without the Reptilian angle, receives over 200,000 visitors daily.

All of these websites achieved much of their traffic following 9/11, with an even greater number of followers coming post the 2007-2008 economic meltdown. What are these websites telling their millions of readers? Setting aside the more extreme conspiracy theories, they are telling us that:

  * Total economic collapse is imminent.
  * The government is controlled by corporate interests
  * Corporations are interested only in profits
  * The mainstream media is controlled by corporate interests

It might be argued that while websites like these have large followings, they lack credibility. However, credibility is in the eye of the beholder. As mentioned, David Icke was once the laughing stock of England. Today, he tours the world, attracting thousands of attendees to his day long lectures wherever he goes. On the other hand, CNBC, "First in Business, Worldwide" has become a laughing stock since the crash, which it completely failed to foresee. As a 2009 Variety article put it: "Credibility is a fragile commodity, and for all its bluster, CNBC's is in tatters." The article went on to tell the story of an eight minute segment on The Daily Show in which Jon Stewart said, among other things: "If only I'd followed CNBC's advice, I'd have a million dollars, provided I'd started with a hundred million dollars."

So what does the future hold in store for us, based on market sentiments as shown in the crystal ball of the internet? In all likelihood, things are going to get a lot worse before they get better, if for no other reason than because we believe they will. Of course, reality will come into play, just as it does in the stock market, when corrections take place. So far, the actions that have been taken to create an economic recovery have not proven themselves to have been of benefit to anyone except, perhaps, the large corporations and financial institutions who received bailout funds. It is doubtful, though, that these trillions of dollars will prove to be anything more than a very temporary "solution" to our global dilemma.

What Are the Solutions to the Curse of the Internet?

As we have discussed throughout this book, the internet's affect on jobs is yet to be recognized on a significant scale. Yes, there have been a few influential individuals who have raised alarm bells. Two of them were, as mentioned in the introduction, Robert Reich and Martin Ford. Another was Bloomberg Business Week's David Huether, who asked this question in 2006, well before the current economic crisis: "Why is manufacturing employment, at 14.2 million workers, at its lowest level in more than 50 years while manufacturing output is at an all-time high?" This was his conclusion:

"Since 2001, with the aid of computers, telecommunications advances, and ever more efficient plant operations, U.S. manufacturing productivity, or the amount of goods or services a worker produces in an hour, has soared a dizzying 24%. That's 72% faster than the average productivity advance during America's four most recent recession-recovery cycles dating back to the 1970s. In short: We're making more stuff with fewer people."

These respected, mainstream commentators are unfortunately yet to be listened to, while the alternate media, which has a large following, but offers few solutions, remains highly influential. The first thing that must be done is to bring wider attention to the public at large about the curse of the internet. Secondly, solutions must be offered: solutions that benefit everybody. Between the twin curses of the internet's and related technologies' direct bearing on job losses, the negative sentiments of the public and the catastrophic results of the orgy of borrowing that led to the current economic crisis, there can be little doubt that we are headed towards a very turbulent future. We face nothing less than a global catastrophe of historically unmatched proportions if nothing is done - and done fast. There are things that can be done, as individuals and as a nation:

Tax Reform

While a strong argument has been made that the U.S. government has become inextricably bound to big business, we are still a nation that votes and our political leaders depend on our votes to get into office. It is within our power to make demands on them. Historically, politicians avoid raising taxes. Individual tax payers resent having to hand over more of their pay to the government and corporations do everything in their considerable power to avoid paying taxes.

If we are going to avoid widespread civil disobedience in the future, we need tax reform. The trouble is, everyone is arguing about it rather than doing anything about it. Raising corporate taxes and taxes on the wealthy is an obvious solution, but it depends on their willingness to pay their taxes. History shows they are not. Nor can they be forced to. However, it should be possible to persuade them to shoulder some of their tax responsibilities. They did it before, as did wealthy Americans:

* In 1961, corporations paid 47.1% of profits in taxes. In 2011, they paid 11.1%

* In 1961, Americans who made a million dollars or more in taxable income paid 43.1% in taxes (adjusted for 2011). In 2011, they paid 23.1%

In 1961, Americans felt they had a comfortable future ahead of them if they worked hard, paid off their home loans and paid their taxes. They were confident that they were getting tangible returns for their taxes in the forms of social security, good schools (in 1961, even many state universities were free), defence, infrastructure and everything else a stable society requires. How do Americans feel today? These startling statistics provide the answer:

* More than 8 million Americans are working part time because they cannot find full time jobs.

* Over 6 million Americans have completely given up hope of finding a job.

* According to the New York Times, in 2009, the wealthiest 5% of Americans possessed over 60% of the nation's wealth while the bottom 80% had less than 13% of the country's wealth.

* Adjusted for inflation, today's middle class workers make less money than their 1971 counterparts.

* Since 2000, the American family's average income has fallen by

5%, adjusted for inflation.

* Today, over 44 million Americans are on food stamps. This is an all-time high.

* Between 2007 and 2009, the median household net worth in the United States fell by a massive 23%, according to the Federal Reserve.

In 2011, Americans feel cheated by a lopsided system that rewards only the very wealthy. We don't need a tax revolution in order to face a brighter future. All that is necessary is a return to something approaching the system of taxation that worked 50 years ago and made America justifiably proud of being the most prosperous, freest country on earth.

It is essential that the corporations who profit the most from the American consumer must pay their fair share of taxes. What good does it do our society if a corporation like General Electric makes $10.3 billion dollars in pre-tax income, but doesn't pay a penny in taxes? This statistic comes from a 2010 article in Forbes, "What The Top U.S. Companies Pay In Taxes" that asks the question: "How can it be that you pay more to the IRS than General Electric?" It's not that GE evades taxes. On the contrary, its "tax return is the largest the IRS deals with each year--some 24,000 pages if printed out", according to the article's author, Christopher Helman.

There are strong arguments against imposing higher taxes on corporations. Among those arguments is the inescapable fact that they are multi-national corporations that simply shift their operations overseas if it is more profitable for them to do so. What is necessary is to close the loopholes that allow them to pay minimal taxes or no taxes whatsoever. There must be a minimum corporate tax that must be paid based on their pre-tax profits.

Corporations don't shift their operations overseas because they want to punish American workers: they do it for purely economic reasons. Not only do they pay lower taxes in other countries, they get cheaper labor and, even more worryingly, transfer ownership of valuable assets such as patents and software to their overseas subsidiaries. The bedrock of the American success story has been the creativity of small business entrepreneurs. In the corporate era since deregulation, this seems to have been forgotten by politicians and the general public. We feel as if we are being held hostage by corporate America. In the political arena, even well-intentioned politicians cave in to corporate interests. In society, the general populace looks to a corporate career as the best way to secure their future and small investors take the easy way out and invest in the largest, most profitable corporations.

Reducing or eliminating payroll taxes and offering incentives to small businesses may help restore the entrepreneurial spirit in America. According to the Small Business Administration (SBA), small businesses:

* Represent 99.7 percent of all employer firms.

* Employ just over half of all private sector employees.

* Pay 44 percent of total U.S. private payroll.

* Have generated 64 percent of net new jobs over the past 15 years.

* Create more than half of the non-farm private gross domestic product (GDP).

* Hire 40 percent of high tech workers (such as scientists, engineers, and computer programmers).

* Made up 97.3 percent of all identified exporters and produced 30.2 percent of the known export value in the 2007 financial year.

* Produce 13 times more patents per employee than large patenting firms; these patents are twice as likely as large firm patents to be among the one percent most cited.

In other words, we don't need to be held hostage by multinational corporations. We can rebuild the country in the same way we built it - through small businesses. Given the right incentives and if we return to the spirit of our anti-trust laws that keep the threat of monopolies in check, we can have a vital, thriving economy again.

Think Locally, Not Globally

Arguing about macroeconomics, complaining about the greed of corporations and writing revolutionary comments to alternative news blogs is not going to help anyone. These are diversions and impotent outlets for confusion and frustration. It will be far more productive if we find solutions first within our individual spheres of influence.

The worst case scenario is that we are facing a depression as bad as or worse than the Great Depression, so a look at what those who lived through that era experienced may give us insight into what we can do to help ourselves, our families and our communities. During the Great Depression, those who were hurt the most were those who were most dependent on wages and those who livelihoods depended on the financial markets. Many rural communities in the United States and to a greater extend, Canada, Australia and other smaller countries, barely felt the effects of the Depression, while in the cities, formerly productive members of society joined the queues in the bread lines or moved to less populated areas to find a market for their skills and labor. Maryland Republican Representative Roscoe Bartlett is old enough to have lived through the Great Depression. He recommends that "those who can, should move their families out of the city".

Not everyone, of course, can or wants to leave the city. The most secure forms of urban employment are skills that are not internet or even cash dependent. A plumber's skills, for example will always be needed. In times of mild to moderate downturns in the economy, people who are skilled in trades often don't even feel their effects. While a handyman or auto mechanic may not make a fortune in boom times, he can survive and even live comfortably when times are hard. If a total collapse comes and no one can afford to pay for his services, barter arrangements can be made. Stockbrokers, real estate agents, web developers and others with cash and internet dependent skills will be hit the hardest in a depression, with very few exceptions. How many plumbers or electricians jumped out of windows when the Crash of '29 came?

If the economy doesn't collapse completely, we are still facing the inescapable fact that the Internet Age is drastically reducing our job prospects. While we view this with dismay, businesses have embraced technology with glee, seeing it as an opportunity to cut overheads in the form of employees and increase profits. However, today's businesses are now facing a completely unanticipated challenge: they are finding it hard to find employees with the skills they need and when they do find them, they are having trouble keeping them. The strategies some forward-looking businesses are using to address this problem may help us find some solutions to our own employment problems in the Internet Age.

It's not as if there aren't enough skilled programmers, software engineers, web developers and other specialists. The kinds of repetitive tasks needed to keep ecommerce going are being outsourced to India, the Philippines and elsewhere around the world. These repetitive tasks, sometimes referred to as "algorithmic," were most in demand throughout the Industrial era. After we entered the Post Industrial Era, a shift began to occur. The advent of the Internet Age has accelerated that shift. There are more than enough algorithmic workers available, but there is a tremendous shortage of creative, problem solving workers. These have been identified as "heuristic workers" and some businesses have taken steps to attract and keep these vitally important employees.

With only 22,000 employees worldwide, Google is the most visited website in the world and one of the most profitable companies of its size on earth. Company founders Sergey Brin and Larry Page attribute much of their success to their Montessori school upbringing. Montessori schools are designed to encourage heuristic rather than rote learning. Students learn by independently exploring the subjects of their choice, not by repeating drills, memorising facts and taking multiple choice tests. Brin and Page use this same model in their business, offering staff an environment that encourages self expression and innovation. Obviously, it works.

More than anything else, this heuristic approach to life offers us our best chance for survival and prosperity in the 21st century. Individually and collectively, we have to start thinking outside the box and find creative solutions that work. For some of us, it may mean learning a trade or skill that is not dependent on the internet. For others, it might mean freelancing online; enhancing existing skills and acquiring new skills as needed to attract greater remuneration. Others might find that forming cooperative communities in rural or semi-rural areas will give them a measure of security while they adapt to the changes that are occurring. Then again, a few lucky job seekers will be able to score a handsomely paying job at Google, Amazon or one of the other internet giants. The solutions are as individual as we are, but they all have one common denominator: we have to set aside expectations based on the past and brainstorm solutions for the present and the future.

The Economist is generally regarded as a fairly conservative publication and not really one we look to for a fresh perspective. However, this "stodgy" British economic journal may have hit the proverbial nail on the head in its print edition of "The World in 2011." Reprinted online, "The year of hope 2.0: Change Americans can believe in?", by Arianna Huffington, founder of the Huffington Post, starts out by saying that 2008 was a year of blind hope that things might get better all by themselves. Then hope dimmed. The "year of hope 2.0", like the "Web 2.0" is a restructuring of hope.

Huffington's article begins by pointing out the hard, cold facts, saying: "Awful statistics—on bankruptcy, unemployment, home foreclosures—flash warnings that the middle class is under assault, and that America risks turning into a third-world nation" - not exactly the stuff hope is built on. After shocking the complacency out of readers, though, she offers solutions. Are they based on some macroeconomic model? Does she recommend a change in government? While she does quote Frederick Douglas, who wrote, "Power concedes nothing without a demand; it never did and it never will" and urges readers to make demands on America's leaders, this was not the crux of her article's message. In a word, the "year of hope 2.0" is based on compassion. It looks "like the thousands upon thousands of acts of compassion taking place all across America— with people reaching out to help their neighbours, even when they are strangers." She goes on to cite the example of Seth Reams, who started a website called 'We've Got Time to Help'. The mission statement on Reams' blog states the following: "This site is dedicated to helping others and in the process helping ourselves." It then goes on to say that if "even 1% of the current un/underemployed people [in Oregon, where, according to Reams, over 500,000 people were out of full time work] volunteered their time for an hour a week that is 5000 hours helping others in need." Just a moment's reflection will tell you that if this movement of compassion and cooperation takes hold globally, the world will face a far brighter future than it faces today.

Back in 1841, the great American essayist and thinker, Ralph Waldo Emerson, wrote Self Reliance, an essay that has uncanny relevance today. "Nothing can bring you peace but yourself. Nothing can bring you peace but the triumph of principles," he wrote, after counselling his readers against looking for self esteem in social status, property or the comfort of being part of a religious or political group. Now, more than ever, we need to think and act creatively, constructively and compassionately. We need to make the transition from the "Me Generation" to a "We Generation." We're all in this together, so let's work together and find solutions that work for all of us. Otherwise, we will never break the curse of the internet.

Appendix

APPENDIX

References by Chapter

It's Not Paranoia if It's True:
How High Tech Creates High Unemployment

Whatis.com. "Luddite". From: http://whatis.techtarget.com/definition/0,,sid9_gci883880,00.html

Washington Bureau Staff. "Rethinking the Luddites" (6 November 2009). From The Economist: http://www.economist.com/blogs/freeexchange/2009/11/rethinking_the_luddites

Isidore, Chris. "Poof: Another 800,000 jobs disappear" (4 February 2010). From CNN Money: http://money.cnn.com/2010/02/04/news/economy/jobs_outlook/

Ford, Martin. "A Jobless Recovery. . . And a Jobless Future?" (2 February 2010). From Huffpost Business: http://www.huffingtonpost.com/martin-ford/jobless-recoveryand-joble_b_445439.html

Reich, Robert. "Robert Reich on Technology's Impact on Job Loss in America" (22 September 2003). From CIO: http://www.cio.com/article/29795/Robert_Reich_on_Technology_s_Impact_on_Job_Loss_in_America

Reich, Robert. "The Great Disconnect Between Stocks and Jobs" (18 November 2009). From Robert Reich's Blog: http://robertreich.blogspot.com/2009/11/great-disconnect-between-stocks-and.html

Liedtke, Michael. "Google Hiring More Than 6,200 Workers This Year" (25 January 2011). From Huffpost Tech: http://www.

huffingtonpost.com/2011/01/25/google-hiring-2011_n_813900.
html

Google investor relations: 2011 Financial Tables: From Google
Investor: http://investor.google.com/financial/tables.html

Stevenson, Tommy. "Now this is just insane (and un-American)"
(27 January 2011). From Tuscaloosa News: http://politibits.blogs.
tuscaloosanews.com/11545/now-this-is-just-insane-and-un-
american/?tc=ar

eBay Annual Report, 2008: From Asiaing.com: http://www.
asiaing.com/ebay-2008-annual-report.html

eBay Annual Report, 2009: From Asiaing.com: http://www.
asiaing.com/ebay-2009-annual-report.html

Metz, Cade. "eBay marketplace reverses revenue shrinkage: Well,
then. The economy must be fine" (20 January 2010). From The
Register: http://www.theregister.co.uk/2010/01/20/ebay_q4_
numbers/

Bailey, Brandon, San Jose Mercury News. "Oracle's Revenue
Rises 18 Percent, but Growth Slows" (18 September 2008).
From iStocAnalyst: http://www.istockanalyst.com/article/
viewiStockNews/articleid/2632900

Brohan, Mark. "Amazon sales and profits boom in 2010" (27
January 2011). From Internet Retailer: http://www.internetretailer.
com/2011/01/27/amazon-sales-and-profits-boom-2010

"Career Opportunities with Amazon". From careerbuilder.
com: http://www.careerbuilder.com/Jobs/Company/
C8H2NL6L8Z865Q111X2/Amazon/

Kary, Tiffany and Sandler, Linda. "Borders Files Bankruptcy, Is

Closing Up to 275 Stores" (17 February 2011). From Bloomberg News: http://www.bloomberg.com/news/2011-02-16/borders-book-chain-files-for-bankruptcy-protection-with-1-29-billion-debt.html

Slideshow (author not cited). "Retail Stores Closing Doors" (23 April 2011). From WalletPop: http://www.walletpop.com/photos/retail-stores-closing-doors/

Heller, Laura. "Borders Files for Chapter 11" (16 February 2011). From WalletPop: http://www.walletpop.com/2011/02/16/borders-files-for-chapter-11/

Robots Creating a Meltdown of Manufacturing Jobs

Bureau of Labor Statistics, Career Guide to Industries, 2010-11 Edition. http://www.bls.gov/oco/cg/cg1002.htm

Hoovers, Manufacturing Sector: http://www.hoovers.com/industry/manufacturing-sector/114-1.html

World Resources Institute: EarthTrends, The Environmental Information Portal: http://earthtrends.wri.org/searchable_db/index.php?step=countries&ccID[]=5&cID[]=190&allcountries=checkbox&theme=5&variable_ID=217&action=select_years

Curious Cat Investing and Economics Blog: http://investing.curiouscatblog.net/2008/09/29/manufacturing-employment-data-1979-to-2007/

"Meet The pi4 Workerbot" (24 December 2010). From MoneyControl: http://www.moneycontrol.com/news/technology/meet-the-pi4-workerbot_508263.html

Roshania, Neema P. "8 Robots That Will Change Your Life" (23 April 2010). From Kiplinger: http://www.kiplinger.com/

businessresource/forecast/archive/8-robots-that-will-change-your-life.html?topic_id=42

Jones, Daniel Christopher. "How the recession remade manufacturing" (2 September 2010). From Business Management: http://www.busmanagement.com/news/manufacturing-sector-recession/

Made How, "How Products Are Made, Volume 2: Industrial Robots". From: http://www.madehow.com/Volume-2/Industrial-Robot.html

Ayers, Robert and Miller, Steve. "The Impacts of Industrial Robots" (November 1981). From Department of Engineering and Public Policy and The Robotics Institute, Carnegie-Mellon University, Pittsburgh, PA 15213: http://www.ri.cmu.edu/pub_files/pub3/ayres_robert_1981_1/ayres_robert_1981_1.pdf

"Robot Types", from RobotWorx: http://www.robots.com/faq.php?question=robot+types

"How robotics and Automation combination can help manufacturing sector in recession". From Youngster: Industrial Robots: http://robotics.youngester.com/2010/09/how-robotics-and-automation-combination.html

"Industrial Robots and Robot System Safety". From U.S. Department of Labor, Occupational Safety & Health Administration: http://www.asimo.pl/materialy/download/robot-system-safety.pdf

"How a Robotic Arm Works?" From Youngster: http://robotics.youngester.com/2010/05/how-robotic-arm-works.html

"Industrial Robotics Principles". From ThomasNet: http://www.thomasnet.com/articles/custom-manufacturing-fabricating/

automation-electronics

"Robot Parts", from RobotWorx: http://www.robots.com/faq. php?question=robot+parts

"Robotic Sensors", from RobotWorx: http://www.robots.com/ robot-education.php?page=physical+sensors

"Basic methods for programming industrial robots". From autokinematics.com: http://www.autokinematics.com/ Programming-Methods.html

International Federation of Robotics (IFR) Statistical Department, Press Release: "Robotics industry is recovering worldwide" (18 November 2010). From World Robotics: http://www.worldrobotics.org/downloads/IFR%20press%20 release_11_2010%283%29.pdf

International Federation of Robotics (IFR) Statistical Department, Press Release: "The Robots Are Coming!" (23 October 2007): http://www.worldrobotics.org/downloads/20071023_Pressinfo.pdf

International Federation of Robotics (IFR) Statistical Department, Press Release: "IFR: Surging demand for industrial robots in 2010: Automotive industry is the driver of the recovery" (14 September 2010): http://www.worldrobotics.org/downloads/PR_2010-09-14_industrial_EN.pdf

Marinelli, Olivia. "From Humans to Robots: The Consequences of Labor Replacement in the Automobile Industry" (20 October 2008). From Dept. of Geology, University of Maryland: http:// www.geog.umd.edu/academic/undergrad/harper/Marinelli_09.pdf

Kobe, Gerry. "Manufacturing 2010" (August 2001). From BNet, Autos Publications: http://findarticles.com/p/articles/mi_m3012/ is_8_181/ai_79007331/?tag=content;col1

"Nissan develops retoolable car body jig" (1 July 1999). From ALLBUSINESS: http://www.allbusiness.com/professional-scientific/scientific-research-development/248282-1.html

"Applications of Robots in the Automobile Industry". From Scribd: http://www.scribd.com/doc/34831790/Applications-of-ROBOTS-in-the-Automobile-Industry

Tu, Abby. "Industrial robots play more significant role in automotive industry" (12 January 2010). From Adsale Industry Portal 2456.com: http://www.adsaleauto.com/eng/feature/details.asp?fsiid=1&fsid=3927

"Robot Application by Industries". From robotmatrix.org: http://www.robotmatrix.org/RobotApplicationByIndustrial.htm

"Robot Safety" (1987). From New Zealand Department of Labor, Industrial Welfare Division: http://www.robotmatrix.org/RobotApplicationByIndustrial.htm

Falling Dominoes: Retail America in Crisis

WSJ Staff. "NBER Makes It Official: Recession Started in December 2007" (1 December 2008). From Wall Street Journal blog: http://blogs.wsj.com/economics/2008/12/01/nber-makes-it-official-recession-started-in-december-2007/

Tisha. "Music-Sharing Site Limewire Must Shut Down Says Federal Judge" (27 October 2010). From American Consumer News: http://www.americanconsumernews.com/2010/10/music-sharing-site-limewire-must-shut-down-says-federal-judge.html

Hudson, Kris and O'Connell, Vanessa. "Recession Turns Malls Into Ghost Towns" (22 May 2009). From Wall Street Journal, Real Estate: http://online.wsj.com/article/SB124294047987244803.html

Bump, Philip. "How The Aughts Killed America's Malls and Newspapers – With One Stone" (29 December 2009). From Mediaite: http://www.mediaite.com/online/how-the-aughts-killed-americas-malls-and-newspapers-with-one-stone/

"Amazon Announces New South Carolina Warehouse" (7 December 2010). From Charlotte Observer: http://www.charlotteobserver.com/2010/12/07/1894803/amazon-announces-new-sc-warehouse.html

"Amazon, Barnes&Noble and Borders Sales Numbers Annual Update". From Foner Books Internet Book Marketing: http://www.fonerbooks.com/booksale.htm

Brohan, Mark. "Amazon sells more e-books than hardcover volumes" (20 July 2010). From Internet Retailer: http://www.internetretailer.com/2010/07/20/amazon-sells-more-e-books-hardcover-volumes

Yousuf, Hibah. "Amazon profit surges 69%" (23 October 2009). From CNN Money: http://money.cnn.com/2009/10/22/technology/Amazon_earnings/

Gomes-Casseres, Prof. Ben, "The History of eBay". From: http://pages.cs.brandeis.edu/~magnus/ief248a/eBay/history.html

Dannen, Chris. "How eBay Plans to Capture Sales from Brick-and-Mortar Stores" (15 December 2010). From Technology Review (MIT): http://www.technologyreview.com/business/26809/?p1=BI

Copyright Penton Media Inc. "Growth Expected in Manufacturing Sector in 2011" (18 October 2010). From Material Handling & Logistics: http://logisticstoday.com/operations_strategy/growth-expected-manufacturing-sector-1018/

Bustillo, Mark. "Wal-Mart Radio Tags to Track Clothing" (23 July 2010) From Wall Street Journal, Business Technology: http://online.wsj.com/article/SB10001424052748704421304575383213061198090.html?mod=WSJ_hpp_LEFTTopStories

Broyles David; Beims, Jennifer; Franko, James; and Bergman, Michelle. "Just-In-Time Inventory Management Strategy & Lean Manufacturing". From Academic Mind: http://www.academicmind.com/unpublishedpapers/business/operationsmanagement/2005-04-000aaf-just-in-time-inventory-management.html

Dixon, Lance. "JIT II®: Creating the Ultimate Customer/Supplier Partnership". From Institute for Supply Management: http://www.ism.ws/pubs/proceedings/confproceedingsdetail.cfm?ItemNumber=10370

International Federation of Robotics (IFR) Statistical Department, Press Release. "Robotics industry is recovering worldwide". From World Robotics: http://www.worldrobotics.org/downloads/IFR%20press%20release_11_2010%283%29.pdf

"Material Handling Robots". From RobotWorx: http://www.robots.com/applications.php?app=material+handling

Other References:

Bureau of Labor Statistics News Releases: http://www.bls.gov/news.release/empsit.nr0.htm

GDP Deflator: http://www.gdpdeflator.com/?gclid=CNqhq8Gn5KUCFccYHAod9nRw2A
U.S. Census Bureau: http://www2.census.gov/retail/releases/current/arts/sales.pdf

Internet Retailer Top 500 Guide: http://www.internetretailer.com/top500/

Wikipedia. Direct Store Delivery: http://en.wikipedia.org/wiki/Direct_Store_Delivery

Alibaba: http://www.alibaba.com/

Alibaba Express: http://www.aliexpress.com/

Realtors Redundant in Wake of the Internet Revolution

Hethcock, Bill. "Real estate job losses spreading"(30 November 2008). From Dallas Business Journal: http://www.bizjournals.com/dallas/stories/2008/12/01/story11.html

Mattioli, Dana. "Real-Estate Pros Go Moonlighting" (13 October 2009). From Wall Street Journal, News & Trends: http://online.wsj.com/article/SB10001424052748704107204574469292369810818.html?mod=googlenews_wsj

National Association of Realtors®. "2010 Profile of Home Buyers and Sellers
Illinois Report" (December 2010). From Illinois Association of Realtors®: http://www.illinoisrealtor.org/sites/illinoisrealtor.org/files/Final%202010%20Profile%20Illinois%20Buyers%20Sellers.pdf

Foreclosure Fraud. "Housing Market Slips Into Depression Territory" (12 January 2011). From 4closureFraud: http://4closurefraud.org/2011/01/12/cnbc-housing-market-slips-into-depression-territory/

Jones, John. "NAR Predicts Number of Real Estate Agents and Brokers Will Decline" (8 November 2010). From DFW Real Estate News: http://www.dfwrealestatenews.com/2010/11/nar-predicts-number-of-real-estate-agents-and-brokers-will-decline/

McCullagh, Declan. "Real estate's Net turf war" ()28 July 2006).

From CNET News: http://news.cnet.com/Real%20estates%20 Net%20turf%20war/2100-1038_3-6099762.html

Lewis, Regina. "The Basics Of Online Real Estate Sales" (3 November 2007). From CBS News.com: http://www.cbsnews. com/stories/2007/11/02/earlyshow/saturday/main3447998.shtml

iNews Staff. " Florida's Biggest REMAX Office Is Shutting Down! REMAX Partners Goes Out Of Business" (12 August 2010). From iNews Business: http://www.realestateradiousa.com/2010/08/12/ remax-partners-goes-out-of-business/

Harris, Jamie. "Employment Index for Mortgage" (29 November 2010): From Latest Business News: http://latestbusiness-news. com/employment-index-for-mortgage-112201.html

The Crash Landing of the Travel Agent Industry

Harrell Associates. "The Internet Travel Industry: What Consumers Should Expect and Need to Know,and Options for a Better Marketplace" (6 June 2002). From Consumer WebWatch: http:// www.consumerwebwatch.org/pdfs/internet-travel-industry.pdf

The History ofr Corporate. "The History of the Large Company Model: Expedis, Inc.". From: http://www.thehistoryofcorporate.com/companies-by-industry/ leisure-and-hospitality/expedia-inc/

"Travelocity.com: A Glimpse Through History" (23 December 2003): From Internet Travel News: http://www.mgast.com/ Internet%20Travel%20News%20-%20Travelocity_com%20A%20 Glimpse%20Through%20History.htm

"Travel Agent Career, Jobs, and Training Information". From Career Overview, Career and Job Search resources: http://www. careeroverview.com/travel-agent-careers.html

"Occupational Outlook Handbook, 2010-11 Edition"Travel Agents". From Bureau of Labor Statistics, US Dept of Labor: http://www.bls.gov/oco/ocos124.htm

Bain, David. "The Online Travel Industry: The 4 Business Models". From Leisure and Sport Review (LASR): http://www.lasr.net/travelarticles.php?ID=312

GLG Expert Contributor. "Google buys ITA - What does it mean for the travel industry?" (2 July 2010). From Gerson Lehrman Group: http://www.glgroup.com/News/Google-buys-ITA---What-does-it-mean-for-the-travel-industry--49286.html

"Site Currently Offline". "More on Trip Advisor Blocking Google": From Hotel Marketing.com: http://www.hotelmarketing.com/index.php/content/article/more_on_tripadvisor_blocking_google

"History of AMR Corporation and American Airlines". From American Airlines: http://www.aa.com/i18n/amrcorp/corporateInformation/facts/history.jsp

Sabre Holdings: http://www.sabre-holdings.com/index.html

"Priceline.com Says Average Christmas-Time Airfare Is Now $422" (12 September 2009). From Travel Industry Wire: http://www.travelindustrywire.com/article50843Priceline_com_Says_Average_Christmas_Time_Airfare_Is_Now_____.html

Rose, Norman L. "Emerging Trends in Wireless Technology and The Global Travel Industry" (copyright 2003). From Travel Tech Consulting, Inc.: http://www.traveltechconsulting.com/wp-content/uploads/2010/03/Wireless_Travel.pdf

Schnuer, Jenna. "Top 10 Mobile Apps for Travel". From Travel Channel: http://www.travelchannel.com/Places_Trips/Travel_

Ideas/Business_Travel/Top_10_Mobile_Apps_For_Travel

"Facebook Travel Applications Guide" (10 July 2007). From Budget Globetrotting: http://www.budgetglobetrotting.com/2007/facebook-travel-applications-guide/

Lardinois, Frederic. "Travelers Love the Mobile Web - But Most Don't Use Travel Apps Yet " (19 March 2010): From ReadWriteWeb: http://www.readwriteweb.com/archives/travelers_love_the_mobile_web_-_but_most_dont_use.php

Dave Carroll. "Story". From Dave Carroll Music: http://www.davecarrollmusic.com/ubg/story/

"Facts about Google's acquisition of ITA Software". From Google: http://www.google.com/press/ita/

Munarriz, Rick Aristotle. "Expedia Shoots Down Google" (9 December 2010) From The Motley Fool: http://www.fool.com/investing/general/2010/12/09/expedia-shoots-down-google.aspx

Bliss, Jeff. "Google Rivals Urge Lawmakers to Oppose Planned ITA Acquisition"(17 November 2010). From Bloomberg: http://www.bloomberg.com/news/2010-11-16/google-rivals-urge-lawmakers-to-oppose-planned-ita-acquisition.html

Kawamoto, Dawn. "Google Reaches Skyward With ITA Software Acquisition" (7 January 2010). From Daily Finance: http://www.dailyfinance.com/story/google-ita-software-acquisition/19539186/

World Travel Market 2010 (original source). "Travel industry recovering from recession, WTM delegates told". From 4Hoteliers: http://www.4hoteliers.com/4hots_nshw.php?mwi=7954

Fabey, Michael. " Airlines expected to exercise capacity discipline in 2011" (5 December 2010) From Travel Weekly: http://

travelweekly.com/article3_ektid225286.aspx

"Positioning Tourism on the Climate Change Agenda" (12 August 2010). From Travel Industry Wire: http://www.travelindustrywire. com/article50785Positioning_Tourism_on_the_Climate_Change_ Agenda.html

Other Sources:

Orbitz Worldwide: http://corp.orbitz.com/

STA Travel: http://www.statravel.com/

The Construction Industry in a Post-Recession, Digital World

Busselberg, Tom. "Construction industry 'brutally hurt'by recession, still not recovering" (16 March 2011). From Davis County Clipper: http://www.clippertoday.com/view/full_story/12376801/article-Construction-industry-%E2%80%98brutally-hurt%E2%80%99-by-recession--still-not-recovering?instance=lead_story_left_column

O'Leary, Kevin. "The Great Recession: Will Construction Workers Survive?" (6 February, 2010). From Time: http://www.time.com/time/nation/article/0,8599,1960639,00.html

"Building a Stronger Future: A New Blueprint for Economic Growth: Quick Facts about AGC's Plan to Rebuild the Construction Industry". From Associated General Contractors of America (AGC): http://news.agc.org/wp-content/uploads/2011/03/Recovery-Plan-Fact-Sheet.pdf

Davidson, Paul. "Obama budget plan could create millions of jobs" (updated 15 February 2011). From USA Today, Economy: http://www.usatoday.com/money/economy/2011-02-15-infrastructure15_ST_N.htm

Walsh, Bryan. "What Is a Green-Collar Job, Exactly?" (26 May 2008). From Time, Health and Science: http://www.time.com/time/health/article/0,8599,1809506,00.html

Painful Death of the Printing Industry

Reyes, Leo. "Declining print media readership blamed for job losses in Canada" (12 November 2009). From Digital Journal: http://www.digitaljournal.com/article/282023

Reyes, Leo. "Century-old Honolulu newspaper prints last issue" (6 June 2010). From Digital Journal: http://www.digitaljournal.com/article/282023

APN New Zealand. "APN to close printing plant, 150 jobs" (19 October 2010). From New Zealand Herald: losthttp://www.nzherald.co.nz/business/news/article.cfm?c_id=3&objectid=10681666

Plucker, Jonathan; Jumphrey, Jack; Holden, Jocelyn; and Chang, Young. "Trend Analysis of Indiana K-8 Library Services Since the School Library Printed Materials Grant" (August 2006). PDF from Center for Evaluation and Education Policy: http://mgrn.evansville.edu/Library%20Report%202006.pdf

Dumpala, Preethi. "The Year The Newspaper Died" (4 July 2009). From Business Insider: http://mgrn.evansville.edu/Library%20Report%202006.pdf

"For Exposure, Universities Put Courses on the Web". From New York Times: http://www.nytimes.com/2010/11/01/world/europe/01iht-educLede01.html?_r=3&ref=education

Bureau of Labor Statisitics, News Release: http://www.bls.gov/news.release/pdf/empsit.pdf

The New Age of Advertising

"America's First Newspaper". From Archiving Early America: http://www.earlyamerica.com/earlyamerica/firsts/newspaper/

"1870-1879". From University of Minnesota, Media History Project: http://www.mediahistory.umn.edu/timeline/1870-1879. html

"Advertising". From History of Graphic Design, 2008: http://www. designhistory.org/advertising_fall_08.html

O'Barr, William M. "A Brief History of Advertising in America" (18 December 2010). From Advertising & Society Review: http://muse.jhu.edu/journals/asr/v006/6.3unit02.html

Wilson, Mark R. "Mail Order," From The Electronic Encyclopedia of Chicago: http://encyclopedia.chicagohistory.org/pages/779.html

"Top 100 Advertising Campaigns of the Century". From Advertising Age: http://adage.com/century/campaigns.html

McClure, Helen. "The Wild Wild Web: The Mythic American West and the Electronic Frontier," The Western Historical Quarterly 31, no. 4 (2000)

Prasad, V. Kanti; Ramamurthy, K.; and Naidu G.M. "The Influence of Internet-Marketing Integration on Marketing Competencies and Export Performance," Journal of International Marketing 9, no. 4 (2001)

Montgomery, Alan L., "Applying Quantitative Marketing Techniques to the Internet," Interfaces 31, no. 2 (2001)

Davis, Tiffany. "Social Media Revolution" (15 June 2009).

From Jacob Morgan, Social Business Advisor: http://www.jmorganmarketing.com/social-media-revolution/

DiNucci, Darcy. "Fragmented Future", Print 53, No. 4 (1999): p32

Kaplan, Andreas M. and Haenlein, Michael. "Users of the world, unite! The challenges and opportunities of Social Media". Business Horizons (2010)

Cole, Alyson. "Individualism in the Age of Internationalism," Michigan Law Review 99, no. 6 (2001)

Learmonth, Michael. "What Big Brands Are Spending on Google." (6 September 2010). From Advertising Age: http://adage.com/digital/article?article_id=145720

Roubert, Jacques-Herve. "Why Digital Agencies Are Indeed Ready to Lead" (12 November 2009). From Advertising Age: http://adage.com/digitalnext/post?article_id=140498

Winsor, John. "The Future of Advertising" (12 July 2010). From Bloomberg Businessweek: http://www.businessweek.com/innovate/content/jul2010/id20100712_542186.htm

Sacks, Danielle. "The Future of Advertising" (17 November 2010). From Fast Company: http://www.fastcompany.com/magazine/151/mayhem-on-madison-avenue.html

Ehrlich, Brenna. "The Old Spice Guy Now Making Custom Videos For Fans Via Social Media" (13 July 2010). From Mashable: http://mashable.com/2010/07/13/old-spice-gu/

Elliott, Stuart. "Client Cutbacks Bring Agency Layoffs" (6 November 2008). From The New York Times: http://www.nytimes.com/2008/11/07/business/media/07adco.html

Edwards, Jim. "BNET's Ad Agency Layoff Counter: 48,832 Jobs Lost" (31 March 2010). From BNET: http://www.bnet.com/blog/advertising-business/bnet-8217s-ad-agency-layoff-counter-48832-jobs-lost/4610

Velotta, Richard N. "Technology, social media changing how tourism leaders market Nevada" (8 December, 2010). From: Las Vegas Sun: http://www.lasvegassun.com/news/2010/dec/08/technology-social-media-changing-how-tourism-leade/

Bomey, Nathan. "Google plans to add jobs in Ann Arbor as global hiring accelerates" (25 January 2011). From AnnArbor.com: http://www.annarbor.com/business-review/google-plans-to-add-jobs-in-ann-arbor-as-global-hiring-accelerates/

Schweizer, Kristin and Rabil, Sarah. "Internet, Emerging Markets to Fuel Ad Growth in 2011" (6 December 2010). From Bloomberg Businessweek: http://www.businessweek.com/news/2010-12-06/internet-emerging-markets-to-fuel-ad-growth-in-2011.html

"Internet to continue as fastest growing advertising medium" (6 December 2010). From UtalkMarketing.com: http://www.utalkmarketing.com/Pages/Article.aspx?ArticleID=19788

"1-ZenithOptimedia, MagnaGlobal raise ad forecasts" (December 6, 2010). From Reuters: http://www.reuters.com/article/2010/12/06/advertising-forecasts-zenithoptimedia-idUSLDE6B50HU20101206

Guyun, Jessica. "As demand rises for tech talent, companies" (20 November 2010). From Sauk Valley Newspapers

Swift, Mike. "Google growing through aggressive buying spree" (19 December 2010). From San Jose Mercury News: http://www.mercurynews.com/business/ci_16878196?nclick_check=1

The Entertainment Industry
Gives Way to the Intertainment Industry

"Napster". From Wikipedia: http://en.wikipedia.org/wiki/Napster

"Confidential Apple music details leaked" (7 June 2003). From BBC News: http://news.bbc.co.uk/2/hi/technology/2971790.stm

Dediu, Horace. "September Music Events: Just the numbers" (1 September 2010). From asymco: http://www.asymco.com/2010/09/01/september-music-event-just-the-numbers/

Dawtrey, Adam. "Spyglass Entertainment merger aims to get MGM lion back on its feet" (8 November 2010). From guardian.co.uk Film Blog: http://www.guardian.co.uk/film/filmblog/2010/nov/08/spyglass-entertainment-merger-mgm-lion

Golum, Rob. "DVD Purchases Slid 16% in 9 Months of 2010, Industry Data Show" (22 October 2010). From Bloomberg: http://www.bloomberg.com/news/2010-10-21/dvd-purchases-slid-16-in-9-months-of-2010-industry-data-show.html

Roth, Daniel. "Netflix Everywhere: Sorry Cable, You're History" (21 September 2009). From Wired Magazine: http://www.wired.com/techbiz/it/magazine/17-10/ff_netflix

Netflix Media Center: http://www.netflix.com/MediaCenter

Lawyers Condemned to Death by the Internet

Lakshmi, R. "U.S. Legal Work Booms in India" (11 May 2008). From The Washington Post: http://www.washingtonpost.com/wp-dyn/content/article/2008/05/10/AR2008051002355.html

Cotts, C. and Kufchock, L. "U.S. firms outsource legal services to India" (21 August 2007). From the New York Times: http://

www.nytimes.com/2007/08/21/business/worldbusiness/21iht-law.4.7199252.html?_r=1

Bloomberg Staff. "Let's Offshore the Lawyers" (18 September 2006). From Bloomberg Businessweek: http://www.businessweek.com/magazine/content/06_38/b4001061.htm

"Occupational Outlook Handbook". From Bureau of Labor Statistics, U.S. Department of Labor: www.bls.gov/oco/ocos053.htm

Timmons, Heather. "Outsourcing to India Draws Western Lawyers" (4 August 2010). From the New York Times: http://www.nytimes.com/2010/08/05/business/global/05legal.html?_r=4&pagewanted=1

News Release: "RR Donnelley Agrees to Acquire OfficeTiger" (20 March 2006). From RR Donnelley: http://www.rrdonnelley.com/News/2006/2006_03_20.asp

Other Sources:

legalzoom.com: http://www.legalzoom.com/

NOLO, Law for All: http://www.nolo.com

Legal Kit Store: http://legalkitstore.com/

LexisNexis: http://law.lexisnexis.com/webcenters/lexisone/

The Demise of the Stock Broker

Smart Money, "The Gloves Are Off", Smart Money Annual Broker Survey 2010, from: http://personal.fidelity.com/misc/smartmoney-annual-broker-survey.pdf. Source: http://www.smartmoney.com/investing/economy/smartmoneys-annual-broker-survey-23119/

Comstock, Courtney. "Everyone's Least Favorite Traders Are The Only Ones Getting Hired Right Now" (15 October 2010). From Business Insider: http://www.businessinsider.com/almost-every-wall-street-firm-is-hiring-high-frequency-traders-right-now-2010-10#ixzz1Jf6bocxV

CNBC, " Man Vs. Machine: How the Crash of '87 Gave Birth To High-Frequency Trading". From: Yahoo News, http://finance.yahoo.com/news/Man-Vs-Machine-How-the-Crash-cnbc-3981690701.html?x=0&.v=1

Securities and Exchange Commission. "Special Study: Electronic Communication Networks and After-Hours Trading" (2000). From: http://www.sec.gov/news/studies/ecnafter.htm#exec

Lepore, Meredith. "5 Possible Regulations That Traders Are Freaking Out About In 2011" (Jan. 7, 2011). From Business Insider: http://www.businessinsider.com/2011-high-frequency-trading-regulation-2011-1##ixzz1JezOo658

Thomasson,Lynn; Barrett, Paul M.; and Mehta,Nina. "What really happened on May 6?" (2 May 2010). From Bloomberg Businessweek: http://www.msnbc.msn.com/id/37274616/ns/business-bloomberg_businessweek/

United States Department of Labor. "Occupational Outlook Handbook, 2010-11 Edition, Securities, Commodities, and Financial Services Sales Agents". From: http://www.bls.gov/oco/ocos122.htm

Indiviglio, David. "Hiring Freezes and Layoffs Begin on Wall Street" (29 September 2010), From the Atlantic: http://www.theatlantic.com/business/archive/2010/09/hiring-freezes-and-layoffs-begin-on-wall-street/63738/#disqus_thread#disqus_thread

Anand, Anika and Comstock, Courtney. "Layoff Carnage Is Back

On Wall Street -- Here's How It Got So Bad Again" (18 October 2010). From Business Insider: http://www.businessinsider.com/what-banks-have-layoffs-2010-10?slop=1#ixzz1Jf4VMMeM

Comstock, Courtney. "JPMorgan Is Shutting Down All Prop Trading Desks" (31 August 2010). From Business Insider: http://www.businessinsider.com/bloomberg-jpmorgan-is-shutting-down-all-prop-trading-desks-2010-8#ixzz1Jf5FWZoO

Carney, John. "Get Ready For The Fixed Income Bloodbath" (27 September 2010). From CNBC NetNet: http://www.cnbc.com/id/39383634

Van Bergen, Jason. "Direct Access Trading Systems". From Investopedia: http://www.investopedia.com/articles/trading/03/020503.asp

Stone, Amey. "Death of a Stock Salesman"(6 April 2005). From Bloomberg Businessweek: http://www.businessweek.com/bwdaily/dnflash/apr2005/nf2005046_9224_db016.htm

JobSearchUSA.org. From: http://www.jobsearchusa.org/jobs/financial-services/stockbroker

CNBC Video, "The All Time High Stock Trade" (7 December 2009). From CNBC: http://video.cnbc.com/gallery/?video=1687475176

Hason, Deborah. "Reaching Out to Generation X and Y Investors" (16 January 2011). From Investment News: http://www.investmentnews.com/article/20110116/REG/301169996

Koba, Mark. "Life After Wall Street Layoff: Different Job, Less Money" (6 February 2009): From CNBC: http://www.cnbc.com/id/29036830/Life_After_Wall_Street_Layoff_Different_Job_Less_Money

Other References:

Getco, Technology & Markets: http://www.getcollc.com/index.php/getco/tertiary/technology_markets/

CoolTrade™ Homepage: https://www.cool-trade.com/Default.asp

TradeKing Homepage: http://www.tradeking.com/

E*Trade Homepage: https://us.etrade.com/e/t/home

Fidelity Homepage: https://www.fidelity.com/

Charles Scwabb Homepage: https://www.schwab.com/

Scotttrade™ Homepage: http://www.scottrade.com/

The Banking Industry Banking on Technology, Eliminating Jobs

Abell, Jeff. "Technology brings banking changes" (21 February 2010). From The Hawkeye Web Edition: http://www.thehawkeye.com/story/PRG10-banking

Chinedu, Igwe Stanley. "Technological Innovations and in the Banking Sector: An Evaluation of the Rate of Diffusion of the Automated Teller Machine". From Academic Leadership Online Journal, Volume 9, Issue 1, Winter 2011 http://www.academicleadership.org/article/technological-innovations-and-in-the-banking-sector-an-evaluation-of-the-rate-of-diffusion-of-the-automated-teller-machine

Onaran, Yalman and Pierson, David. "Banks' Job Cuts Reach 121,000 as Credit Woes Spread: Table" (26 September 2008). From Bloomberg: http://www.bloomberg.com/apps/news?pid=newsarchive&sid=apSGgutpX6f4

Goldsmith, Julian. "Bank job losses: Offshoring not to blame" (18 August 2008): From silicon.com: http://www.silicon.com/ management/cio-insights/2008/08/18/bank-job-losses-offshoring-not-to-blame-39272475/

Heath, Nick. "Credit cruch boosts outsourcing" (18 June 2008). From silicon.com: http://www.silicon.com/management/cio-insights/2008/06/18/credit-crunch-boosts-outsourcing-39248272/

Forrester Research: http://www.forrester.com/rb/research

Malik, Abdul Rahman. "Outsourcing it Positions to Low Cost Countries" (22 June 2007). From Associated Content: http://www. associatedcontent.com/article/290561/outsourcing_it_positions_ to_low_cost.html

Ho, Shirley J.and Mallick, Sushanta K."The Impact of Information Technology on the Banking Industry: Theory and Empirics" (2006). From: webspace.qmul.ac.uk/pmartins/mallick.pdf

Son, Hugh. "Bank of America to Close Some Branches, Test Remote Video Wealth Advisers" (10 February 2011). From Bloomberg: http://www.bloomberg.com/news/2011-02-10/bofa-to-trim-bank-branches-test-remote-video-wealth-advisers.html

"Security First Network Bank". From Wikipedia: http:// en.wikipedia.org/wiki/Security_First_Network_Bank

King, Brett: "Bank 2.0" From: http://banking.crossmedia-integrierte-kommunikation.de/files/2010/10/Bank-2.0.pdf

"ING Direct". From Wikipedia: http://en.wikipedia.org/wiki/ ING_Direct#ING_Direct

"HSBC Direct". From Wikipedia: http://en.wikipedia.org/wiki/ HSBC_Direct#HSBC_Direct

Shinai, John. "Companies Plan Increased Offshoring" (4 February 2011). From FINS Technology: http://it-jobs.fins.com/Articles/SB129683052338783155/Companies-Plan-Increased-Offshoring

Rosenberg, Jim. "Why has M-PESA become so popular in Kenya?" (17 June 2008). From CGAP: http://technology.cgap.org/2008/06/17/why-has-m-pesa-become-so-popular-in-kenya/

Globe GCash, "How it Works": http://site.globe.com.ph/web/gcash/how-it-works?sid=TaKDp8uxpRcAAC@M5IkAAACde

Breaking the Curse of the Internet

"Real U.S. unemployment rate may be 22.1 percent for February" (06 March 2011). From EU Times: http://www.eutimes.net/2011/03/real-us-unemployment-rate-may-be-22-percent-for-february/

John Williams's Shadow Government Statistics: http://www.shadowstats.com/

"Losing the Information War: Is the US really losing the information war, as Hillary Clinton claims, and how can it fight back?" (06 March 2011). From Al Jazeera: http://english.aljazeera.net/programmes/insidestory/2011/03/20113675732489765.html

"Hillary Clinton: US Losing Information War to Alternative Media" (04 March 2011). From GRTV: http://tv.globalresearch.ca/2011/03/hillary-clinton-us-losing-information-war-alternative-media

Gustin, Sam. "Social Media Sparked, Accelerated Egypt's RevolutionaryFire" (11 February 2011) From Wired: http://www.wired.com/epicenter/2011/02/egypts-revolutionary-fire/

Kelleher, James and Bailey, David. "Largest crowds since Vietnam

War march in Wisconsin" (26 February 2011). From Reuters: http://www.reuters.com/article/2011/02/26/us-wisconsin-protests-idUSTRE71O4F420110226

Faber, David. "The Bubble Decade" (date not cited). From CNBC: http://www.cnbc.com/id/33972968/

Tancer, Bill. "Will The Housing Bubble Burst in 2007?" (22 February 2007). From Time: http://www.time.com/time/business/article/0,8599,1592751,00.html

W3SPY.net: http://w3spy.net/

Lowry, Brian. "CNBC: Cheerleading Nitwits Bluster Cluelessly" (09 March 2009). From Variety: http://weblogs.variety.com/bltv/2009/03/cnbc-cheerleading-nitwits-bluster-cluelessly.html

Freed, Judah. "CNBC credibility blasted on The Daily Show" (05 March 2009) From Examiner.com: http://www.examiner.com/media-industry-in-national/cnbc-credibility-blasted-on-the-daily-show

Huether, David. "The Case of the Missing Jobs" (03 April 2006) From Bloomberg Businessweek: http://www.businessweek.com/magazine/content/06_14/b3978116.htm

valerb. "Interesting tax and income information from 1961 and today" (15 April 2011). From Silverseek Forum: http://forums.silverseek.com/showthread.php?46523-Interesting-tax-and-income-information-from-1961-and-today

The American Dream. "Broke And Getting Broker: 22 Jaw Dropping Statistics About The Financial Condition Of American Families" (30 March 2011). From Prison Planet: http://www.prisonplanet.com/broke-and-getting-broker-22-jaw-dropping-statistics-about-the-financial-condition-of-american-families.html

Helman, Christopher. "What the Top U.S. Corporations Pay in Taxes" (01 April 2010). From Forbes: http://www.forbes.com/2010/04/01/ge-exxon-walmart-business-washington-corporate-taxes.html

Office of Advocacy. "How important are small businesses to the U.S. economy?" From U.S. Small Business Administration: http://www.sba.gov/advocacy/7495/8420

Slavo, Mac. "Congressman Warns: 'Those Who Can, Should Move their Families Out of the City'" (28 May, 2011). From the Intel Hub: http://theintelhub.com/2011/05/28/congressman-warns-%E2%80%9Cthose-who-can-should-move-their-families-out-of-the-city%E2%80%9D/

Huffington, Arianna. "The year of hope 2.0" (22 November 2010). From the Economist: http://www.economist.com/node/17493282

We've Got Time to Help: http://wevegottimetohelp.blogspot.com/